∞

33 Years in the Holy Land

A. G. SERTILLANGES

33 YEARS
IN THE
HOLY LAND

What Jesus Saw
from Bethlehem
to Golgotha

Translated by L. M. Ward

SOPHIA INSTITUTE PRESS
Manchester, New Hampshire

33 Years in the Holy Land was formerly published under the title *Christ among Men* (London: R. and T. Washbourne, Ltd., 1908). For this 2019 edition by Sophia Institute Press, the first chapter of the original edition has been omitted, and minor editorial revisions have been included.

Cover by David Ferris Design.

Cover image: *The Entry into Jerusalem*, Master of the Thuizon Altarpiece, fifteenth century, © Bridgeman Images (TRK2961968).

Scripture citations are taken from the Douay-Rheims Version of the Bible. Where appropriate, quotations have been cross-referenced with the differing names and enumeration in the Revised Standard Version.

Nihil obstat: J. P. Arendzen, *Censor Deputatus*
Imprimatur: Gulielmus, Episcopus Arindelensis, *Vicarius Generalis*
Wesmonasterii, April 11, 1908

Sophia Institute Press
Box 5284, Manchester, NH 03108
1-800-888-9344

www.SophiaInstitute.com

Sophia Institute Press® is a registered trademark of Sophia Institute.

Library of Congress Cataloging-in-Publication Data
Names: Sertillanges, A.-D., 1863-1948, author. | Ward, L. M. (Lilian M.), translator.
Title: 33 years in the Holy Land : what Jesus saw from Bethlehem to Golgotha / A.G. Sertillanges ; translated by L.M. Ward.
Other titles: Jésus. English
Description: Manchester, New Hampshire : Sophia Institute Press, [2019] | "33 Years in the Holy Land was formerly published under the title Christ among Men (London: R. and T. Washbourne, Ltd., 1908)."
Identifiers: LCCN 2019002453 | ISBN 9781622826605 (pbk. : alk. paper)
Subjects: LCSH: Jesus Christ—Biography. | Palestine—Description and travel.
Classification: LCC BT301.3 .S4713 2019 | DDC 232.9/01—dc23 LC record available at https://lccn.loc.gov/2019002453

First printing

Contents

∞

Author's Preface

In the following pages we submit to our readers a few thoughts about Jesus.

On returning from a voyage to the country of the Gospels, our heart filled to overflowing with memories of His earthly life, we cannot resist the impulse that was born of our admiration, our reverence, and our love, and in this spirit we have written this little book. At the present day, men speak much about Christ—men who know Him little and men who secretly hate Him. Indeed, we may truly say it is not always in a right or honorable spirit that they refer to this sacred subject. Some there are who, not being convinced as to the divinity of Jesus, extol, if we may so speak, to excess the splendors of His humanity. God knows we do not wish to question the sincerity of these men, but, on the other hand, there are some who glorify His humanity only in order to stifle and smother His divinity beneath the weight of His human perfections. We pity these poor deluded men, and we must do our utmost to undo the evil they do. We, however, must not ignore the beauty of the humanity of Jesus, just because other men write falsely about it. In Jesus, all is admirable and sweet, beautiful and instructive, reflecting the transcendent glory of the Soul from which it emanates.

One thing we must ever remember: that the Man was made only to give us the God, that the exterior beauty of His human life was only the reflection of His divine existence, so that, in a word, He was, in His human nature and in His human acts, as the nave of the Temple, which leads us to the altar of His Godhead.

∞

Preface to the English Edition

The work that is here presented to the public is intended to promote the science of the saints as taught by the words and example of our Divine Savior during His life upon earth. It is a translation of a French work written by the Abbé A. G. Sertillanges after a visit to the Holy Land.

It has been the endeavor of the translator to give the exact teaching of the author, and his descriptions of localities and of customs, in a style suitable to the taste of English readers. The subject treated is the most sacred and important that can interest and benefit the pious reader — namely, Christ among men, or characteristics of Jesus as seen in the Gospel.

In reading the Old Testament, we find the majesty and greatness of God presented before us, and our souls are impressed with reverence and the fear of His Name and of His judgments. Therein we are forcibly reminded of the following truths:

> The Lord is terrible and exceeding great, and His power is admirable. (Ecclus. 43:31 [Sir. 43:29])

He hath made a decree, and it shall not pass away. (Ps. 148:6 [149:5])

Great is the Lord, and great is His power: and of His wisdom there is no number. (Ps. 146:5 [147:5])

O Lord, our Lord, how admirable is Thy Name in the whole earth, for Thy magnificence is elevated above the heavens. (Ps. 8:2 [8:1–2]).

The New Testament reveals to us the charity and tenderness of God, in order that our souls may be moved to correspond to His grace and to return love for love. It is from the Gospel that we learn how much God has loved, and how He has proved His love by becoming man, by living our life, and by giving His precious blood for our redemption. In the Gospel, we are told of the poverty of Christ, of His work, of His teaching, and of His death upon the Cross, and we are taught that all this is the effect of divine love. "For God so loved the world as to give His only begotten Son, that whosoever believeth in Him may not perish, but may have life everlasting" (John 3:16).

The more we study the Gospel and meditate upon it, the better shall we learn the lesson of the love of God, as that is revealed in its every page, by the words and actions of our Savior. It contains the history of the Son of God upon earth and tells us what our souls desire to know: What does the Son of God wish? What does He seek upon earth? Why did He come into this world in poverty and lowliness? Why did He pray and preach? Why did He work and perform miracles? Why did He suffer and die for us?

It was because, as the psalmist says, "He hath set His tabernacle in the sun, and He came as a bridegroom" (Ps. 18:6 [19:4–5]).

His love astonished earth and Heaven. He became man through love, and in wonder we can think of God poor through love, despised and neglected for the sake of love; reduced through love to the extremities of dereliction and cold indifference, signified by His own words: "The foxes have holes, and the birds of the air nests; but the Son of Man hath not where to lay His head" (Matt. 8:20). He came and dwelt among us to give an example of virtue and sanctity, to teach us how to live as the children of God in every stage of life, from the cradle to the grave: "I have given you an example, that as I have done, so you do also" (John 13:15); "Be ye therefore perfect, as your Heavenly Father is perfect" (Matt. 5:48); "Take up my yoke upon you, and learn of me, because I am meek and humble of heart; and you shall find rest to your souls" (Matt. 11:29).

He knew that men could not imitate God as He is in the throne of His glory, and as revealed in His incommunicable attributes, and therefore He would teach us how to imitate Him in humility and patience, in poverty and suffering, in prayer and communion with Him, in our dealings with our fellow beings, and in our estimate of nature and of grace—of the natural and the supernatural order of things—that in our being, both here and hereafter, the words and predictions of John may be verified: "Dearly beloved, we are now the sons of God: and it hath not yet appeared what we shall be. We know that when He shall appear, we shall be like to Him, because we shall see Him as He is" (1 John 3:2).

These are some of the reflections and ideas suggested by the reading of this devotional book. Each chapter contains subject matter sufficient to impress our souls with reverence and admiration, and to supply food for pious meditation.

The plan of the work is arranged in such a way as to secure the purposes for which it was written, dealing with certain parts of Christ's life and showing their characteristics in a manner that can be imitated by His followers in the corresponding stages of their lives.

We are told how our Lord conducted Himself at each stage —namely, in childhood, in His hidden life at Nazareth, in His life of prayer and preaching, in His interactions with men, both friends and enemies, and in His relation to the whole universe. Each chapter has been written with a view of placing before us our Lord's behavior as recorded in the Gospels under the peculiar circumstances and surroundings of His life, so that it may appear easy for Christians of every age, and in their own circumstances, to copy His example and to walk in His footsteps.

There is another feature of this book that calls for special attention—namely, the geographical outlines, and the descriptions of the Holy Land and of the holy places sanctified by the presence and the wonderful works of the Son of God made man. No one can read these without obtaining the knowledge of places and circumstances that is such a help to meditation and spiritual reading. Happy are those who can visit the holy places in Judea and Galilee, who can kneel at the tomb of their Redeemer and there renew their communications with Him; and grateful must those be who, not having had that privilege, are enabled to read the records and the account of the experience obtained, and the devout sentiments inspired by pilgrimage to or dwelling in the Holy Land.

The work of translation has been carefully and accurately done, and the translator may be congratulated on her achievement in this, as in her former work, *The Suffering Man-God*, in rendering the French original into an English version clear and intelligible to every class of readers. She will have the goodwill and prayers of the many devout souls who ever look with earnest eyes to the example of Christ, and who will readily welcome an account derived directly from the Gospel records of how He lived His earthly life among men.

—Arthur Devine
Passionist
St. Savior's Retreat
Broadway, Worcestershire
Feast of the Purification, 1908

∞

33 Years in the Holy Land

Chapter 1

∞

The Cradle of Jesus

∞

Of all the circumstances in the earthly life of Jesus, the most
charming, the tenderest, and the sweetest to the Christian mind
are those that we recall, with a crowd of happy memories, at the
sound of the magic name of Bethlehem.

All of the Master's life can be epitomized in these few words:
Bethlehem, Nazareth, the Lake, Jerusalem. Nazareth signifies
mystery and silence. The Lake signifies work. Jerusalem signifies conflict and suffering. Thus was His life as one long day,
with its work and its burdens, its silence and its pain. In the
day of Jesus, Bethlehem is the morning — the fragrant fresh-
ness of dawn, the first smile of Heaven, the gentle breeze that
exhales new life and gives forth perfumes rich and rare, such as
we dream of when contemplating the first fair Paradise where
man was made.

Bethlehem! What glad rejoicing rings in that name! It awak-
ens echoes of angels' songs and the soft fluttering of their wings.
When our hearts pronounce that happy word, we hear once
more in fancy the peals of Christmas bells and gladly recall our
childhood's joys. But, at the same time, our reason tells us that
we may discover many lessons here.

God's time had come for fulfilling the hopes of His people, but
He looked not on the great or mighty ones, not on the religious

or political chiefs of the earth. He chose from a poor, despised village a humble child called Miriam, or Mary.

Mary was like those young girls who may be seen nowadays at Nazareth, on the road to the fountain, grave and modest of mien, and clothed in the traditional costume of the women of her race, which consisted of a many-colored tunic, a white veil, and a girdle around her waist, with one hand holding her pitcher, filled at the well, and her other hand drawing her veil around her.

This was the instrument God chose for the accomplishment of His designs.

And while this child of scarcely fifteen prayed in her humble dwelling beneath the rock, God sent an ambassador to her from His throne in Heaven, one of those great beings who, in spite of their superior nature, do not disdain to associate with the human race, for the glory of their Father and ours. The angel made known his request, and, Mary's consent being given, the mystery was accomplished. Heaven bowed down and filled the earth with hope in filling a bosom with mystery and a heart with love.

After some months, the edict of Tiberius came forth. A census must be taken; all must set out to their native place to be enrolled. Joseph, the pure spouse of Mary, was of the family of David; Bethlehem, the city of David, was therefore the place to which he must go to enroll himself.

The hour seemed ill chosen, for the time was close at hand when Mary would give birth to her Child; but the proud emperor paid no heed to the inconvenience and pain he caused.

Mary and Joseph set out on their journey — a journey of four or five days. Probably they were equipped just like the travelers one meets in the present day in Palestine. The Virgin was seated on a donkey; at her side walked Joseph, with his staff and cloak, and carrying a few provisions for the journey.

The way they took was the same as they traveled over three times a year for the feasts: the Plain of Esdraelon, Nablus, and Jerusalem. Each evening, they halted at inns, which were always open to travelers on entering a village or town. This was an old established custom; men and beasts rested there, generally beside a stream, and the next morning, having no one but God to thank for the hospitality, they continued their journey. Often the pilgrims who crowded this route at the times of the festivals sang psalms and canticles in praise of the Zion to which they were journeying.

Perhaps Mary and Joseph felt their hearts were too full to imitate them; but if their lips were silent, they chanted within their souls their glad Magnificat of happiness and love.

They arrived at Jerusalem and walked along the walls on the west side, near the fortress; then, crossing the plain and the hills, which echo today with the cries of Rachel's sorrow, in a few hours they reached the little city of David. Let us pause for a moment and describe this country where Bethlehem rises in the midst of bare mountains, like a flower springing out of the rocks. Outside Jerusalem—that city of whiteness besieged by the desert on the east and bounded by the Kedron and the terrible Gehenna—Bethlehem stands on a hill. It is like an amphitheater, surmounting a deep valley that is truly a "land of plenty." Thus was it called Ephrata, "the fruitful," cultivated by the industrious inhabitants in the form of long terraces covered with fig trees and clinging vines, which traced beautiful designs on the white soil.

Bethlehem was the much-loved dwelling of Solomon. He it was who first made the gardens that spread out at the foot of the town, in the little valley of Artas. Above, near the road to

Hebron, he built vast reservoirs, which still exist. They were filled from a hidden spring in a subterranean grotto, which was called the Sealed Fountain, and the valley below was known as the Closed Garden, signifying the names given by Solomon to his spouse in the Song of Solomon (see 4:12). These reservoirs, just mentioned, supplied water, by means of pipes, to the dwellings in the Holy City, so that the life of Jerusalem may be said to have sprung from thence, even as the Life of the World came forth from Bethlehem.

And Bethlehem of today has its charms. When, having climbed the little hill, one stands in the picturesque public place that is the center of life in Bethlehem, he faces the sacred grotto over which now stands the most ancient basilica in the world. Then, glancing over the white tombs of the cemetery, which serves as a border on the crest of the hills, one sees below him the fertile, terraced gardens leading down into the Valley of the Caroubiers.

A little beyond, resting on the mountain, rises the village of Beit Sahour, whence came the shepherds, and the country of Boaz, in whose fields Ruth the Moabite was wont to glean (see Ruth 2:8). To the right of the horizon lies the Dead Sea; to the left rises Jerusalem, the city of blood. Memories sweet and sad are roused within us as we see in the marketplace, among the rows of camels bending under their loads, young maidens with long white veils—sisters of the Virgin—and graceful children in many-colored dresses, toward whom our hearts go out with a feeling of tenderness, while thinking of their brothers—the Holy Innocents—and of their other Brother, Jesus. Thus is the soul filled with many conflicting thoughts of joy and sorrow. Strange feelings overwhelm us, and many pictures pass through our minds, some sad and others happy; and still in the center of all lies the crib, the cradle of Jesus, which prefigures so much pain, and out of which must rise the Cross.

But let us rest here till the shades of evening fall, and our impressions will be still more wonderful. For to *us* Bethlehem is night; it gained its value to us at midnight; it is the silence of the world; it is Nature quiet and at rest; it is the beautiful hill rising under the magic starlight, to draw from Heaven its well-beloved. And when face-to-face with the reality with which we delight to outline our dreams—sitting among those tombs, so white that they recall to us the tears that Jesus shed there, and thus their very sadness is charmed away—we see the shadows fall, then rise by degrees and hover above us, till noiselessly each star shines through, while beneath us the bleating of the flocks rises in the soft warm air and seems like a cry from the plain, a sigh of the night. We feel our hearts throb with gladness, and, turning to the little cave, we cry out, "It is there!" and our souls exult and are filled with joy. The present exists for us no longer, and in our happy dreams we hear sweet voices of the past, which, while uttering nothing, tell us so much. Pausing here, we will watch the Holy Group arrive, weary and footsore after their tedious journey, but calm and happy withal.

It is toward evening when Mary and Joseph reach their journey's end. They have been preceded by several of their compatriots, travelers from all parts of Judea; and, consequently, as Bethlehem is a small town, there is no room left for them in the inn. We know how beautifully the Fathers of the Church apply this fact to us. They tell us that the crowded inn is like the human heart. There is room for many things, many people, many interests. Like the Oriental shelters, always open to the passersby, we ever welcome what comes with an attractive and pleasing appearance. The crowds rush in; they overwhelm, they absorb us. A crowd of thoughts, of desires, of earthly plans, of business, of passions—all find room. And when Jesus comes, He comes too late. Sometimes we fear to entertain such a Guest.

He is exacting and troublesome, is Jesus Christ! When He comes, He wants His abode to be clean, honorable, undisputed. How can He lodge beside some of the guests we have admitted? And so we say to Him, "Go hence!" Oh no, we do not say so with our lips, it is true; but our hearts are more eloquent than our tongues, and our hearts say plainly to Him, "Go hence! There is no room for you. Leave us in peace. Begone!" And Jesus goes away, and we remain with our miseries, like the inn at Bethlehem, which might have sheltered the Infinite, but would not.

Behold Mary and Joseph without lodging, wandering through the streets of Bethlehem, harassed by the dangers of the night, and overshadowed by the dread hour that was approaching! We may guess the anxiety of Joseph, his eagerness, and his trouble. This is all so hard, so unexpected. As for Mary, when we recall the touching preparations that mothers make for the birth of their firstborn, we may imagine her sorrow. And yet her great tranquility was not disturbed by the faintest shadow of doubt or uneasiness. She bore within her the Director of all things, He who knows all, who can do all. To be uneasy with regard to Him would be foolish. As to herself, what could anything matter? Had she not all things in having her Treasure? When she thought of the supreme honor that had been conferred on her, could she envy rich mothers who live in luxury? To suffer with Jesus within her was a double joy. It was to begin the work of expiation, the work of the Savior. It was to carry the Cross in carrying Him who was to be nailed to it. The Mother of Sorrows began there her heavy duty, and we can imagine with what an immensity of tenderness she did so, when we recall to what an extent Mary was associated in this great work, and consequently how fully she partook in the universal joy it brought to men.

Mary went on and on through the narrow streets of Bethlehem, without fear, without anxiety. She was awaiting the will of God, and God poured into her soul, drop by drop, His serenity and peace — serenity greater and deeper than that of the still, dark night that rose now from the plains, and closed slowly over the beautiful hilltops.

What ineffable exchanges were being accomplished: Mary giving Jesus His blood, His life, the beatings of His heart; Jesus giving ·Mary light, strength, love, patience, and that peace that comes to those who possess God. Thus, conducted by her spouse, led on more surely by Providence, sitting on the poor weary beast whose hoofs sounded on the stone pathway, as a cry scorned and unheeded, Mary went on her way silently, hiding Heaven under her downcast eyelids and shielding with her white veil her heart, which contained her God.

Anxiously, patiently, diligently Joseph sought for shelter, and found none.

At length, travel-stained and weary, having abandoned all hope of hospitality from men, he remembered other shelters that were not closed against the poor. Under the hill near the Tower of David were a number of grottos, such as may be seen in all parts of Palestine, but especially in Judea. Here the shepherds sheltered their sheep, but at this time of the year, as the flocks were at the pastures on the hillside, the caves were empty. Joseph, remembering this, directed his steps toward them.

Providence directed their feet, for it was ordained that the Son of God should find shelter where He would not be the Guest of any but God. Like an ever-watchful mother, Providence has a retreat and shelter for all who live; she hollows the caves in the midst of the forests and forgets not the son of the lioness. When, in the beginning, she presided over the evolution of matter, and when her workman, fire, solidified the shapeless globe, she reserved this grotto, this little cave of Bethlehem, in anticipation of the hour of God's coming.

It was not fitting that Divine Immensity should be enclosed in the dwelling of man; that He, the rich Sovereign, who rules the sun and commands the dawn to break, who brightens the darkness with stars and throws over the night a mantle more gorgeous than that of kings, should be born in the midst of vain riches and perishable grandeurs. He overcame all earthly pomp in scorning it. Of His own choice, He showed Himself to us in what the world would call misery. He would have no luxury other than what became Him as the Restorer as well as the Creator of the earth. Flower of the world, but not flower of the soil, He would bloom and grow in the midst of His creation, choosing for His place of birth a cave that had had no other architect or decorator but God His Father, to whom He was equal in all things.

And was it not meet that He who became man for all should, from the hour of His birth, be accessible to all, especially those who most resembled Him: the poor, the little ones, the scorned of men, but beloved of God?

See! The shepherds come from the borders of the desert of Judea, their heads covered with dark veils, with sheepskins thrown over their shoulders, and clothed in simple, rough tunics, holding staffs with which to guide the straying sheep. These are the men whose guest Jesus chose to be. They are of no importance in the eyes of men. In the East, more than anywhere else, they are servants of the servants themselves, having no home but the caves and rocks, like Him whom they welcome to earth. It is to them that Jesus offers Himself.

They are in the plain guarding their flocks or gathered around their fires, and silently Jesus invites them. Immediately they obey, without doubt, without fear. Be they now shepherds or kings, their rights are equal; they both can gaze on, love, adore, and, if they dare, even hold in their arms the Son of God, for they are simple and clean of heart.

Thus, Heaven urges the weary travelers to enter the cave. There is no earthly temple here to enclose the Real Presence; but Nature offers her temple to welcome her God. The dome is formed of rugged rocks. The altar is a crib. Mary and Joseph enter, and the hour for which Heaven awaits approaches. The poor lodging that Joseph endeavors to make more fitting offers its lowly resources to the hidden God. And the holy spouse, humble and filled with awe, retires into his nothingness in the vision of the Infinite about to come on earth.

Bethlehem slumbers; Nature is still. The stars look down and softly twinkle. The angels, happy and expectant, with hymns of joy upon their lips, await their Master's signal to break forth in songs of jubilee.

All is ready. The mystery may now be accomplished.

Chapter 2

∞

The Hidden Life of Jesus

∞

Whoever seeks to penetrate the life of Jesus will there discover, even in the midst of the agitation and turmoil of His active life, retreats full of silence, where His interior life reposes in tranquil radiance, and of which His public life is but the veil. For that which characterizes His thirty years of obscure, and apparently useless, existence is that its very hiddenness is alone all that is visible to us.

Upon Nazareth the Gospel is dumb; at Nazareth all is mystery and silence. As Moses in the cloud, conversing alone with God, so was Jesus in His hidden life. And perhaps it is bold of us to try to penetrate that cloud.

At the time of Christ, Nazareth was a little hamlet, lost in the mountains of Galilee — the Galilee that was despised by the priests and great ones of Israel. "Can any good come out of Nazareth?" say they (see John 1:46).

And, indeed, it was a place of little importance. Three or four thousand souls; a synagogue, to which, perhaps, was attached a small school; and that was all — neither commerce, nor a garrison of Roman soldiers, none of those large houses that gained a reputation of gaiety, and, one must also say of corruption, as in Tiberias and Magdala. Even less could Nazareth pretend to possess one of those famous schools that, in some places, were built in the shadow of the Temple and were the pride and glory of a Jewish city.

Situated twenty-five leagues from Jerusalem, nine hours' journey from Capernaum, far from the frequented way, Nazareth was little known and seldom noticed. She was like the rose spoken of by St. Jerome that opens her chalice only for Heaven.

Today the pilgrim who comes from Jerusalem will find the little white village hidden, like a dove's nest, among the summits of the hills that rise above the Plain of Jezreel. When, on the other hand, one approaches it from the north, coming from Galilee, it appears in a hollow, for it lies hidden in one of those upper valleys that are so common among the pasture hills of Palestine. When one arrives there, with the spirit animated by memories, and the soul filled with the personality of Jesus and His hidden life, which is but suggested to us in the few words in the Gospel; when one considers what He was and what He is, the terrible mysteries locked up in His soul, the eternity of His existence, the infinity of His work, and the immensity of His Name, one pauses in reverent awe.

See this village, these houses, with their flat roofs, like blocks of white stones on the green slope; the narrow street hollowed out of the mountain, on either side of which flourish all the life in the little city — this is Nazareth! Here was passed the hidden life — thirty years of that life of which each moment could have saved a world. O God! how small are Thy immensities! And the spirit, for a moment stunned, feels suddenly within it a delight at these happy memories, these familiar images.

What! Was it *there* that Jesus lived? *There* that the Treasure of the world reposed? And did He pass thirty years, hidden from men, even as is this little village lost among the mountains, humble among the humble, exposed to rebuffs, to common surroundings, and gaining His livelihood by the labor of His hands? Yes, my God, yes!

Jesus Christ did not come into this world for Himself: He came for our sakes—to suffer and humble Himself for us, to be degraded and die for us—that was His intention in coming. And Nazareth was but a step on the way to Calvary; and because it was a step to Calvary, it is a wondrous encouragement and a sweet consolation to those who have here, on earth, their Calvary. The humble, the little ones, those who in this world find only misery and obscurity—each of those can say: "He has been poor; He has been humbled, like me, and for my sake"; and this humiliation suffered in company with Jesus becomes sweeter, and the journey is less weary when the end of their cross is rested on the Master's shoulder.

When we contemplate what was the great humility of Jesus as man, must we not worship it as a glory of Jesus as God?

What are our human conditions to God? Our wealth and greatness, our position and our advantages—what are they in His sight? Poor little flies that strut about and despise other flies because their wings are a little less bright or their feet a little less dainty—what are you worth? Great or small, in God's eyes your value depends only on how far you correspond to the graces suitable to your condition, and truly to Him the humblest is the most worthy of honor. Thus does He signify His indifference to worldly pomp. Ignoring the nothingness of our glories, He shows forth His own glory.

Looking at Nazareth, how can vain thoughts arise within us? The human condition of the Savior here shines forth with a divine brilliance. And this poverty, willingly chosen, draws in its train eternal riches; this annihilation is the paving to that glorious home of the Infinite beyond the stars.

We have entered Nazareth; we have walked along its narrow street to this poor house—can it be called a house?—where lived in silence the Man-God. It is a cavern hollowed out of the rock, with a stone structure joined to the entrance. Today it is a chapel, and devout souls can pray in the dim vault, and priests can call God down to earth, renewing, after two thousand years, the Real Presence.

Ah, what a flood of thoughts rushes in on us! The past rises before us; the rough walls speak to us, while Heaven seems to bow down, in very love, to shelter and hide this sacred spot. They lived here! They loved thy shade, O rock! They led here, peacefully, the life of those peasants so often seen in the villages of the East, hidden in their humble homes, far from our civilization, ignorant of our schemes and our problems, but near Nature and near God.

Mary was here. She went twice each day to that fountain, the very same where the maidens now go to draw water, wading in the clear pool. With bare feet, she modestly advanced with her companions, carrying her pitcher and waiting her turn, which perhaps was long in coming. Then, filling her pitcher, she returned carrying it on her shoulder. She did her simple household work with the Infinite in her heart. She lighted the fire in a hole in the rock, and cooked their frugal food—food for the Lord of the universe! She baked the bread earned by Joseph and Jesus! And the angels bowed down in loving admiration of God's purest creature.

Ah! how truly are those deserving of pity who are scandalized at this simplicity and who say, "Was that all?" Yes, indeed, *that was all*; and you—are you more than this? Your grand dresses, your jewels, your luxury and civilization, your ignorant and arrogant science—do you fancy that these things make any impression on God? And your dreams of wealth and greatness—what are they to Him, who is the Lord of all things?

Perhaps, O worldling, you would have chosen as Mother of God a distinguished person instead of a barefooted virgin? You would have selected for His home a palace instead of a grotto in the rock? The Creator of Heaven saw no shame in this. It was all equally great in the eyes of Him before whom all is so small; and since His heart desired to stoop to His creatures, it was a joy to Him to stoop as low as was possible to Infinite Love.

How can we describe those thirty years passed in the obscurity of Nazareth?

They were a preparation. Jesus Christ did not need any preparation for Himself. The great problem of *vocation*, so difficult to others, and more or less slowly solved, was anticipated in His case. From the first moment, conscious of Himself, He knew what He desired, and He could realize it, if He so pleased; but such was not His design. He wished to wait for *man's* time. His divine authority must have, for visible support, His human authority. Therefore, He waited patiently while, in man's time, His body according to the flesh was being developed.

Must we understand from this that those thirty years were devoid of any result with regard to His divine work? No; we must guard ourselves emphatically from thinking this.

Jesus Christ came into this world to give Himself, to speak a word, to show an example, and to die. His death will come. It is not yet time to preach His word, but there remains the giving of Himself and the showing of an example—the example of humility, of patience, of submission to God and to those who represented Him on earth. And the gift of Himself to whom? To

His Father, in the first place. And we must notice that this act is truly the vocation of Christ. Is He not, through His atoning death, the ransom for sin? Is He not the price of the guilty and the intercession of the just? And that Voice that cries, "Behold, I come to do Thy will, O my God!" (Heb. 10:9)—is it not the expression of all redemption and all the priesthood in Christ and, consequently, of all His work on earth?

The rest is a surplus—a wonderful surplus—of love, of condescension, of justice; but in the simple cry "Behold, I come" all redemption is contained. This cry was ever coming from the heart of Jesus—at Nazareth as on the Cross.

St. John the Baptist said to those who came to question him: "I am the voice of one crying out in the wilderness" (John 1:23). Jesus Christ is the voice that calls to God. And all that He is, and all that He can do—all His thoughts, His feelings, His aspirations, His joys, and His pains; all the breath of His lips and the beatings of His heart—all cry out to God; *all* supplicate, petition, intercede, make reparation; *all*, coming from a Divine Person, possess a divine value, and the world is saved, because Jesus the Savior lived and died.

And thus, in giving Himself to God, Jesus Christ gave Himself to men. In the quiet Temple of Galilee, in this humble home, where the atmosphere was silence and speech was used only for the praise and service of God, Jesus gave to the world His Real Presence. Like the winter's sun, radiant and tranquil, rising on a world frostbound and dead, giving no heat, not causing the earth to fructify, but seeming to come only to brighten and rejoice the heart—so was Jesus.

When we visit these places where Jesus lived, they are sanctuaries. The hills are the altars; the trees, the flowers, the rocks, the light clouds are a sublime decoration for this shrine, where

Heaven stooped to dwell. There is between these objects and those entirely profane all the difference that our ideas form between the marble pillars of a temple and the stones covered with dust by the roadside.

For truly, Nazareth is a temple. It is the ark that enclosed the living law of the Most High. It is the golden candlestick that held the Light that enlightens the world. It is the rock whence flows the Living Water that floods and purifies the earth.

What did Jesus do at Nazareth?

The Gospel answers us: "He advanced in wisdom and age and grace with God and men" and also tells us, "He was subject to them" (Luke 2:51–52).

It cannot be expressed with a more sublime simplicity that Jesus did not distinguish Himself visibly at Nazareth from those around Him. He willed that His deeds should resemble ours, in order that our merits might be like unto His. As a child, He played with those who later were called the "brethren of Jesus" (see Matt. 12:47) — that is, His cousins and other children of the village. Doubtless the little ones played as we see them play today, for the East changes little in its customs — at marriage feasts and funerals, or at fashioning little birds of clay, a favorite game of the Oriental child. These childish games form part of that picture of the "glory, full of grace," of which St. John speaks in the beginning of his Gospel (see 1:14).

As He grew older, He had the ordinary interactions with His neighbors, distinguished only by the perfection of His life, but so similar to others that even His relations did not know who He was. This was proved later by their opposition and their murmurs. The glory of the midnight hour around His divine cradle had been so secret in its grandeur that none guessed who had come. A veil of silence enshrouded the Well-Beloved. Faith alone, in the twilight of sweet memories, taught Mary and Joseph the truth about Mary's Child. Doubtless they prayed together. Like all the Jews, they prayed for the redemption of Israel. Who can fathom the sentiments of piety in that holy group? What union of hearts! What looks of timid, rapturous adoration from Mary and Joseph! What loving abandonment on the part of Jesus! He was silent about Himself, and they understood the silence. Ah, those happy hours were divine, and they wished they might never end. But His life—when He must act—was waiting, and day followed day in rapid procession, each passed in prayer, in study, and in labor.

Study! Strange word to apply to Jesus! And yet we must remember that Jesus, while truly God, was really man, and had in consequence an intellect capable of progress, in the sense that knowledge depends on experience and on the spontaneous labor of the mind. The knowledge that is specially styled human would, in a perfect degree, be as inappropriate to the *mind* of Jesus as a child as would the features of a man and the walk and voice of a man be to His childish *body*.

In some sense, He learned nothing from man. He loved to read the Scriptures, where He found His Father's name, and His human knowledge increased; but in reality all knowledge came from Himself.

From the age of five, all Jewish boys began to learn verses from the Bible. At ten, they were taught the rabbinical traditions, written later under the title Mishna.

On Sabbath days and feast days, during the long leisure hours passed in their homes, the Jews occupied themselves thus. In a number of towns, there was a small school attached to the synagogue. Each master had charge of not more than twenty-five children, whom he instructed, chiefly by asking and answering questions, as did the Divine Master Himself in His public life. He taught them to read from the rolls of parchment on which the law was written, and to write with the *calam*—in the beautiful characters of Holy Writ—passages of the Bible that it was judged good for them to know, such as the history of the Creation, the Canticles of the Feasts, and the Law of Moses. Finally, this course of education was completed by practical lessons on the manner of behaving in the different circumstances of life—a sort of study in politeness and in the customs in vogue among the Jews.

Thus did Jesus pass the first twelve years of His human life. Having arrived at that age, a new career opened itself before Him, because that was the age appointed for entry in the social life among the Jews. He was then admitted to the honor of worshipping in the Temple, and He went for the first time to Jerusalem. Jerusalem! We may easily guess the emotion that vibrated through the soul of Jesus when passing through its gates and entering its Temple for the first time.

This was that famous edifice where, amidst the confused clamor of idolatry, His praises had resounded for centuries. Here were offered those sacrifices—flowing with the blood of their victims and accompanied by prayer and incense—that were the figures of His own great Sacrifice; and His heart was stirred to its infinite depths—that heart so tender and sensitive, so ready to embrace all that touched His Father's honor.

When the Levites and their sons intoned the psalms (after the great libation of the Passover), it was, so say historians, like one great voice of thunder, which shook the very foundations of the Temple and echoed even to the valley of the Kedron. Jesus must have mingled His voice with theirs, and together they repeated those holy words of the psalmist: "Behold, I come to do Thy will, O my God!' (see Ps. 39:8–9; Heb. 10:9). We will not pause long over the one episode that marks the first visit of our Divine Lord to the Temple. Jesus in the midst of the doctors is a foreshadowing; His teaching is an earnest of that wisdom that later He will show to men. The bold words of Mary, "Son, why hast Thou done so to us?" (Luke 2:48), are a commentary on those other words of the Evangelist, "He was subject to them." And, again, the Savior's response, "Did you not know that I must be about my Father's business?" (Luke 2:49), was the summing up of His whole life. Thus, in this one incident, we see Him entirely—His life and work, as it were, epitomized in one bright flash of light, the essence of the light invisible. But His hour had not yet come. The Star returned to the shadows of the night until it was to arise in all its brilliance and illumine the world.

Let us return with the Holy Family to Nazareth, and there contemplate a new wonder: Jesus working for His bread. From the days of His infancy to the days of His public life, Jesus worked. He had need to work, for Joseph's was a poor house. This was another burden He took upon Himself as the Son of Man.

An Israelite who did not learn a trade was despised. "It is as if he were taught robbery," said the rabbi. All worked with their hands, however high their calling. Hillel was an engraver on wood; Shammai was a carpenter. Some even did not consider it beneath them to work as shoemakers, tailors, smiths, or potters. The practical and laborious spirit was ever a characteristic of the Jewish nation. Even today in the Eastern cities, the contrast between the activity of the Jew and the resigned indolence of the fatalist Muslim is remarkable.

Then, again, in the labor of Jesus there was a special significance, as the calling of Him who came "not to be ministered unto, but to minister" (Matt. 20:28) and who would, at one and the same time, obey the law and sweeten labor, thus showing us a double example.

Work is a virtue, and it also sows the seeds of virtue, for it alienates the suggestions of evil, inasmuch as it uses our energies, both of body and of mind; it brings us in closer intercourse with our fellow creatures; it does more for the great social question than do those empty strings of phrases in which rich, idle men lament the unhappiness of the present day while they do not perceive that they are themselves a social wound, an object of envy and scandal to their brethren, a dead spot in the great living organism, an obstacle in the race of human life.

Thanks be to God, these men are not the greater portion of the human race. Work is the ordinary condition of man. It is for this reason that Jesus, who came to teach *all*, gave the world this striking example. Christ was a working man during the greater portion of His life.

And what kind of work did Jesus do? Tradition is unanimous in telling us that He worked as a carpenter. We can picture Him at work, as we look at the little joiners' shops in the narrow streets of the Arab quarter at Nazareth, mere grottos formed by the hollows in the rocks. They worked on the bare ground, half in shadow, half in the light, with arms and legs bare; sometimes making yokes for the oxen or ploughs for the fields, holding the wood in place with their feet, or sometimes neatly fashioning little rails and frames with that primitive tool they called the drill bow, under which the slender splinters curled and shone like sheaves of pale gold touched and colored by the sun. We are told that Jesus worked thus, only He was graver, more modest, more silent than His companions; for was not His work of greater value than theirs?

The contrast between these humble labors and Him who deigned to perform them was so stupendous as to cause His work to become a solemn and religious ceremony. We are awed in spite of ourselves, and are hushed in contemplation of this silent work, and in wonder at the motives that directed this humble labor. We forget ourselves as we pause and gaze upon the Divine Workman working silently, without haste, in a corner of the little shop. We watch His hands, and then we look up and see His eyes, and there His soul beams forth with a tranquil radiance, and the little shop and Nazareth and all the world is flooded with a glorious, celestial light.

We are raised and crushed and utterly overcome with a delightful sense of peace as these thoughts come over us.

The labor of Jesus was not incessant, not always heavy; we can conclude this from the character of His people and of the time in which He lived on earth. It would be incorrect to picture in a shop in the East the feverish excitement that prevails in our countries. This difference is, in great measure, due to the difference in climate. Also, our energies are exerted to their full extent in an almost frenzied manner to meet our requirements, real or imaginary. It is not so, however, in the East.

On the Sabbath and feast days, all work was suspended. What did Jesus do then? We have already said: He prayed, He read the Scriptures, and He meditated on them. He went onto the flat roof of His little home, or onto some neighboring height, and prayed. How often, perhaps, He climbed one of those little hills that overlook Nazareth, where all the surrounding country lay before Him, and all the roads over which His Apostles would travel.

To the north, the chains of Lebanon, with Hermon crowned in snow. To the east, the Sea of Galilee, partially veiled by the intervening hills, the future theater of so many divine manifestations. To the south, Gilboa, the hills of Endor, of Jezreel, and, further still, the mountains Ebal and Gerizim reminded Him, with the Plain of Esdraelon, of the wars and great deeds of His ancestors. Close to Him, Tabor offered Him a throne for His glory, and at His feet lay the white tombs of Carmel.

We may imagine what passed through the mind of the Master; and when at evening, the horizon shrinking in the gloom of coming night, He saw around Him the winnowers with their wooden buckets casting the grain on the summer wind, the laborers returning from their work, flocks of sheep rising like white clouds of dust, and the watchmen taking up their posts of guard; when the sweet scent of the almond and the lemon tree was wafted to Him on the gentle breeze—oh, then, how sublime must have been His reverie!

His imagination was flooded with those beautiful pictures that His parables have bequeathed to the world. And in all Nature—charming, restless, and at rest—Jesus read the Name of His Father, discovering in all creation the sublime symbols that veil, yet show forth, His beauty and His truth.

Later on, as the time drew near for Jesus to manifest Himself to the world, He retired more closely into His solitude. He gave Himself for the world, but His wisdom fixed the limit and the time. He showed Himself, acted, spoke, cured, consoled, exhorted, and was all things to all men; but when His work was done, His interior life recalled Him, and He retired alone. "He went into the mountains alone" is told again and again in the Gospel (see Mark 6:46; Luke 6:12). For days—sometimes many days—at a time, He was sought and could not be found;

the desert or the mountain were His safe retreat. Behold Him there, in a shady nook beneath the spreading trees or in a lonely grotto open to the sky, His soul rapt in ecstatic union with God.

His soul carried always with it a great solitude, even in the midst of work and tumult; but at times, He sought visible recollection for our edification and instruction, and as an example to His disciples.

We must learn to be recollected, as He was. Whatever our solicitudes may be, we must lead an interior life, where the distractions and cares of business cannot enter, or at least cannot penetrate to the injury of the soul. We have exterior duties, but we must always be careful to remember that they are worth only what they are worth in the Master's eyes. Our labors — what are they in themselves? The toil of our hands, the work of our brains — what are they to God? For this is all that counts. And if we or others reap the fruit of our endeavors, what are these fruits worth if they do not lead to life eternal? When we and they have passed away and the balance of life is closed, what will remain? Only God and our value in His sight.

We must, then, love and nourish our souls, and, to this end, we must seek recollection and solitude. Solitude calls God to us; it opens our hearts to higher thoughts, and casts us into those depths within ourselves whence our manly resolutions spring forth, and where our best impulses arise.

Again, the hidden life is a great example. Thirty years.... Three years. Three years of action; thirty years of silence, of labor, of obscurity, of obedience. The obedience of God to those He placed over Him, to the circumstances directed by His hand; the detachment of Himself from the world — that is to say, evil and false maxims, false glory, false love — these were the glories of Christ, and they must be ours.

The Hidden Life of Jesus

Our life is not usually a life of incessant public display; it is in great measure a hidden life. To permeate it with the spirit of Christ at Nazareth will be to inundate it with peace, to give it a divine serenity, for it will give us the security of seeing Him in that land that is promised to us as the reward of our labors here.

Chapter 3

∞

The Preaching of Jesus

Nazareth, we have seen, was a preparation; that is, the great work of redemption was still to be accomplished. The time now drew near when Jesus, who came to restore humanity, would work visibly for the realization of this great design. He must first rouse the truth lying dormant in the souls of men, then teach them; first conquer the empire of sin, then exhort and lead aright; first draw men to God with the chains of love, then reveal that same love to men, in order to make them know their Heavenly Father and inspire them with confidence in His goodness.

The public life of Jesus had this threefold end. And that is why one day the little cottage of Joseph was deserted, and the Son of Man showed Himself to the world.

The Gospels tell us how Jesus began His public life. He went to the bank of the Jordan to be baptized by John. He who instituted Baptism would be the first to give the example in the New Law. He desired to sanctify by His touch those waters that were to serve for the regeneration of His children. He elected to cleanse in His pure flesh the defiled and sinful flesh of the sons of Adam.

Jesus went forth from Nazareth, turning to the east, and descended to the bottom of that great valley where the Jordan rushes down from the north, and where, as in a sepulcher, four hundred feet below the Mediterranean, lies the Dead Sea. There

He received the testimony of John and the testimony of the Eternal Father. He descended into the waters of the river that, traversing the greater part of Palestine, created life as it flowed, even as He Himself created the life of the world. After His Baptism, Jesus once more climbed the solitary heights that surround Jericho, desiring to remain alone for forty days, thus entering His active life by the avenue of silence.

The solitudes chosen by Jesus were those in which the prophets of Israel used to fortify their souls, where the Precursor, weakened by fasts and visited by visions of the Messiah, rested and passed the nights in prayer, after having spent the day baptizing and instructing. Jesus retired there in order that He might draw Himself into closer contact with His Father before commencing His great work. There He fasted, and subjected Himself to the assaults of the enemy, who did all in his power to thwart our Divine Master in the task He had undertaken. And, gazing into the future, He embraced with His all-seeing eyes the work He was about to do. Like the sun, mentioned in the psalm, penetrating the earth, "He rejoiced as a giant to run the way" (Ps. 18:6), longing to reveal His soul, rich with the riches of the Infinite, and to pour His graces into the souls of men.

Again, after forty days, He returned to the banks of the Jordan, and, mingling with the multitudes that came from all parts to hear the preaching of John, He preached His word.

Three questions rise in our minds in connection with the preaching of Jesus:
  • Where did He preach?
  • In what manner did He preach?
  • What were the chief characteristics of His preaching?

In the first place, the "theater" of the apostolate of Jesus was the country bordered on the north by Lebanon, on the east by

the mountains Moab and Gilead, on the south by the Dead Sea
and the desert, and on the west by the ocean. It was a country
about the size of Switzerland. According to St. Jerome, it was
sixty leagues in length and scarcely twenty leagues in breadth. So
small was it, indeed, that this great doctor feared to describe it,
"lest," he said, "he should lay himself open to the blasphemous
sarcasms of the pagan." Truly there is something strange, even
confounding, in the thought that such an immensity as was the
life of Jesus was confined in so small a space.

In two days' journey, we can travel from end to end the
country where Jesus lived; and yet it is of Him that it is written: "Thou art my Servant, to raise up the tribes of Juda, and
to gather the lost ones of Israel; I have established Thee to be
the Light of nations, and to carry my name to the ends of the
earth" (see Isa. 49:6).

What a contrast between the immensity of this task and the
apparent narrowness of the scope in which to accomplish it!
When we are told that the brethren of Jesus, marveling at His
works, said to Him, "If Thou canst do these things, show Thyself
to the world" (see John 7:4), we are tempted to say they were
justified in speaking thus. How was it that Jesus, "the Universal
Man," could consent to confine His whole life to this one small
place—one little portion of the universe?

And yet it appears to us that in this circumstance, instead
of a scandal, we can discover one of the most divine traits, if we
may dare to say so, in the Master's conduct. God delighted in
this prodigy, which consisted in causing immensity to bud forth
from obscurity—the great tree from the tiny grain. He created
all things out of nothing, in order that nothingness might bear
testimony to His power; and as He created the natural world, so
did He form the supernatural.

33 YEARS IN THE HOLY LAND

God could have sent His Christ to all quarters of the globe; He could have prolonged His earthly life until the end of the world; but He preferred to reduce that life to a short space and a narrow field of action. Thirty-three years—or, rather, three years—was the length of time; Palestine, the smallest country of the world, was His field of action. Space and time do not count for anything. What God chooses, that alone counts.

God willed that Jesus should not leave His beloved Judea. He confined Himself to this little square of land, taking months to traverse this little country of a few days' journey. But when He had spoken His word and left an example, He told His Apostles to go and conquer the entire earth.

The Apostles! Would it not have been more than folly, were it not commanded by the All-Powerful, for them to go and conquer the world? Fishermen, a tax collector, and a carpenter—such were the poor men whom Jesus had called to His side one day from their business, and who often did not understand the meaning of His words. How well He knew them! He knew He could not depend on them, and He warned them not to trust themselves. But, He added, "I will send my Spirit" (see John 15:26). And it was the Spirit who would regenerate the world. It was the *spiritual* presence of Jesus, not His corporal presence, that was to accomplish His work. That was why He lived without anxiety and died without fear. Men grow anxious because they are not the masters of time; they wish to accomplish everything themselves, because they are not the masters of others, and they cannot rely on others to complete their work in their way. Jesus Christ is the Master of man and time. His earthly life was only a flash of light, His native land a small place on the universe;

but from this little place this flash of brightness shone forth and illuminated the entire earth.

In fact, may we not confine the theater of the preaching of Jesus to a still smaller space and say that the true birthplace of the Gospel was Galilee, and the lake known as the Sea of Galilee—places more dear to a Christian soul than even Jerusalem itself, and to which we always turn as to our native land?

When the pilgrim approaches Galilee after the weary journey through the desert, it seems like turning back the pages of history: each step he takes is a step back into the twenty centuries that are past, till at last he feels he is living in the days of Jesus. It was there that the New Law was proclaimed. Seated on a rock, with the crowd pressing around Him, some standing, some sitting, on the grassy terraces that lead up from the lake, He spoke, and, touching their hearts, taught them of Heaven.

In those days, about a dozen small towns surrounded the little sea. How often He passed from one to another, crossing the waters—which were sometimes smooth and tranquil, sometimes agitated by storms—to go to Capernaum, known as *His* town, or to Bethsaida, Chorazin, and Magdala, wherever He would save a soul or preach His doctrine.

Today silence reigns over these waters. Desolation is spread as a cloak over the land, and it is as though no profane reality dare interrupt the dream—the living presence of a Man-God. Hardly a trace of life: a boat, a few fishermen mending their nets, as in the days of Andrew and Simon Peter; a gypsy tent, and, shrouding all, a melancholy calm. All seem to be but phantoms, living symbols, whose only excuse for being there is to give color to a dream.

How can our feelings be earthly and commonplace when treading these hallowed spots? Here, where the very silence is an act of adoration, where all life is but the memory of a far-off smile, where each year, lovingly, Nature, in her ever-recurring anniversaries, keeps holiday, filling the valleys with gay blossoms, and charging the soft, warm air with fragrant perfume; here, in the actual place where Jesus lived, our souls exult, rejoice, are overwhelmed with gladness. We revel in the memories of the past, and centuries return to tell their tale. Once more we hear, floating on the soft, still air, that gentle, mysterious voice: "Blessed are the poor.... Blessed are they who suffer.... Come to me, and I will give you rest" (see Matt. 5:3, 10; 11:28–29).

We hear the divine accents across the wall of centuries, and we whisper to our hearts with loving reverence: "At this moment, from all races of humanity, the crowd of souls who read the Gospel turn to this spot where we—more privileged than they—may walk; their dream rests upon this lake over which our boat now glides. We feel the breath and hear the sighs of those who have gone before, borne across the calm blue sea." I recall a day when, sitting on the heights of Gadara, a little hill overlooking the lake a mile distant, I watched one of those glorious sunsets that seem to contain and give forth all the splendors of the East. Slowly the sun sank, as though resting on the violet clouds that rose from the earth. The lake lay beneath, and the setting king of day, radiant and calm, inundated it with its tranquil splendor. Far on high the glory was lost in the infinite heavens, while to right and left it spread over mountains and hills and broke the horizon with a luminous glow, till the world from end to end seemed lighted up with one undying fire. My heart rose joyously within me, and the cry burst forth, "Here is Christ!"

He passed His life within this narrow space. Like the sun, which seemed at that moment to belong to the lake, for as it sank lower, it shone only on the water, yet which, at the same time, was illuminating the whole world—so was the life of Jesus. He trod these paths. He stood on Tabor, rising before me. He spoke here, lived here, and here He gathered around Him the poor, the blind, and the lame. In reality, He spoke to the whole world, He lived for the whole world, He cured the whole world. What matter that this hallowed spot is only a little corner of the universe? The *place* is of little matter. His actions extend over infinity, and He spoke to all men and all ages when He addressed the little groups on the borders of the lake and charmed the sinner by His gentle word.

Secondly, in what manner did Jesus preach? He might have come—as, indeed, He was expected—a great Lawgiver and Master, bearing in His hands a learned code, a complete doctrine drawn up and explained, embracing all the ends and objects of life. But no, He did not come like this. No written code, no complete system, no learned dogma. He showed *Himself*, and He told men that *He* was the Law, *He* was the Truth. He let men gaze on Him, and behold! they were taught; He acted, and, again, they learned the law; He spoke, and all doctrine was contained in His word. He seemed to speak as if without special care, as circumstance demanded, but, in truth, all the ordinary life of man was directed from His short apostolate.

Each Saturday, in all the more important towns of Judea, the people assembled in the synagogue; they prayed together, and they read the Bible, upon which one of the more learned among those present was invited to preach. Jesus made use of this custom, and a passage in St. Luke's Gospel relates to us what happened (Luke 4:14–22).

It was a Sabbath day at Nazareth, and Jesus, clothed "in the power of the Spirit ... went into the synagogue, according to His custom." The people, after the usual prayers, waited for the reading of the word of God, when a young man rose from the crowd and desired to speak. It was Jesus the Carpenter. How great must have been the surprise of all present! No man is a prophet in his own country, as our Savior Himself said. Little was known of Him, in spite of His preaching, beyond the fact that He had not studied under any earthly master, and yet He seemed to be more learned than His comrades.

However, the chief of the synagogue gave the desired permission, and Jesus mounted the pulpit—a kind of platform on which the Bible rested—and receiving from the attendant's hands the book of Isaiah the prophet, He unrolled it, and read: "The Spirit of the Lord is upon me, wherefore He hath anointed me, to preach the Gospel to the poor. He hath sent me, to heal the contrite of heart; to preach deliverance to the captives and sight to the blind, to set at liberty them that are bruised, to preach the acceptable year of the Lord and the day of reward." Then He paused, and, closing the book, began to commentate. "The eyes of all in the synagogue were fixed upon Him," St. Luke tells us; they waited to hear what He would say. And, breaking the heavy silence, He began: "This day is fulfilled this Scripture in your ears." And with an eloquence full of dignity He explained the doctrine that in Him the empire of sin had been conquered. "And all gave testimony to Him, and they wondered at the words of grace that proceeded from His mouth, and they said: 'Is not this the son of Joseph?'"

Frequently Jesus traveled over the country of Galilee, preaching and curing as He passed, gathering souls to Himself, and calling them from beside the fountains, in Jerusalem, in Solomon's porch of the Temple — wherever He went, He had His disciples. More often, He would go to the shores of the lake, and sitting on a rock or standing in a boat, He would open His heart to His people and draw them closer to Himself. In every manner and in every place, by answering their questions, by the events of His life, by the cures He effected, the testimonies He received, the opposition He met with, the conversions He made, all He said and did — He cast the seed of truth abroad and showed to men the beauty of His thoughts, His sentiments, His entire Being. It was truth itself, which reposed as in a furnace within His human form; truth, which burst forth bright and life-giving when He conversed with men.

As with the "theater" of Jesus' preaching, so was the preaching itself: He did not disquiet Himself seeking to travel over the whole earth, nor did He explain His doctrine in all its bearings and remote conclusions. What need had He of erudite systems or methods? Why should He try to explain all things in one short apostolate? He is the living Authority that gives forth truth and doctrine as circumstances demand. And this Authority, which showed itself, as it were, in one short flash and then eclipsed itself at the Ascension, remains ever-watchful, perfect, and eternal. "Behold, I am with you all days, even to the consummation of the world" (Matt. 28:20). We understand His word. The Church, that society that He founded, is, after Him, the living authority. Continuing His mission, working under His command, teaching in His Name, she also, according to the circumstances of the lives of her children, formulates that which they must believe as well as directs what they must do. We may say, in passing, that this authority is what condemns the errors of our separated brethren. True, they adore the Gospel, but they refuse to submit to this divine authority, not realizing that the written Gospel is but one lamb from the Fold of Christ, and that this Fold itself in which Jesus abides is the Catholic Church.

All is contained in this work of God. The power of Jesus overflows on all sides the narrow limits in which He seems to be confined; and a wisdom, an infinite calm, which are none other than Divine, govern the organization of the plan that directs the life and welfare of the whole earth.

It is a colossal trap, built all of love, with which He ensnares the universe.

The chief characteristics that distinguish the preaching of Jesus may be reduced to two: namely, simplicity in its profoundness, and its persuasive strength, which results from the divine nature of Him who speaks, His character, and His life. Simplicity and profoundness — these two features are inseparable in describing the preaching of our Divine Master. He was in Himself the Wisdom of God. He came to enlighten the human race, to draw it to Himself, the Infinite Good, and to lead it to its supernatural home. In Himself, Jesus was a living mystery, and yet He desired to make Himself known to men. Thus, necessarily, His teaching must be profound.

On the other hand, He addressed Himself to the ignorant and the simple. Different from the Pharisees, who despised the poor and ignorant, and denied them even the credit of being virtuous; different from the men of genius, who, pretending to reform the minds of men, addressed themselves only to the educated, and neglected the less enlightened, Jesus became, and lived as, a man of the people. He gave as a sign of the divinity of His mission the evangelization of the poor. He spoke so that the simplest might understand. The groups who gathered around Him — and of which the more noted were Peter, the fisherman; James, the carpenter; and Matthew, the tax collector of Capernaum—would not long have followed intricate or learned controversy. It was necessary for the Infinite Wisdom of God to stoop to the weakness of His creatures.

If we read His discourses, we find that they are all, except on very rare and special occasions, full of a simplicity that is even royal. This, indeed, is their most striking characteristic: royal simplicity. We know that kings, in speaking to their intimates, are so simple as to be even disconcerting. Kingdoms, scepters, and crowns are no more to them than are ordinary, everyday objects to us. Thus, Jesus, the King of Kings, spoke with tranquil simplicity when speaking to man of His kingdom and power.

His eloquence was naturally sublime, because the source from which it sprang was divine; it was also spontaneous and natural, without show, exaggeration, or excitement. In reading the prophets, who discoursed on similar subjects, we are struck by the contrast. They tortured themselves in trying to give forth the impressions that came upon them from without. They were ravished and transformed, following the wild, strange flights of the spirit into regions of superior light. But Jesus carried the light within Himself, and it shone forth naturally. He had no need to endeavor to penetrate regions of mystery. The mystery was in Himself; the mystery *was* Himself, and He disclosed the mystery in showing Himself to men.

In all preaching, one quality is necessary. If the word spoken is to have any hold on the people to whom it is addressed, it must be living and proved. A crowd of people is like a child. They must be spoken to in images, comparisons, and figures. The Oriental especially delights in bright touches and living similitudes. The rabbis of that day knew this well. The Talmud is full of these images. They are only spoiled by their pedantry and by their excessive subtlety. Jesus Christ, in curing this abuse, reestablished the custom in its perfection. He adopted the bright, crisp style, the living image, the incisive manner, and the beautiful, familiar comparisons.

He did not make use of fables—they contain an element of error and of childishness that is repugnant to divine things—but He adopted the *parable*, a transparent veil gently folded around a truth, which it hides and discloses at the same time. He used the parable because it stimulates the imagination and the feelings in a calm, efficacious manner to receive the hidden truth, whether joyous or grave, and therefrom to draw salutary conclusions.

In His parables, He did not paint scenes that were foreign to His hearers or fantastic. He took His images from real facts of everyday life and from objects always before their eyes: the mountains, the cities, the tombs, and the fountains. He taught them by the corn, by the flowers of the field, by the pastures green and ripe. The white lambs and the black goats, separated from each other in the pastures, served as a picture of the Judgment; the vineyards and their workers represented the vineyard of His Father; and the barren fig tree by the roadside also taught a lesson. All Nature rose up, so to speak, and flocked reverently to Him, that it might enter into that marvelous pulpit of His teaching, even as we are told the branches of the trees on the road to Egypt bent down to worship Him while He passed on His first journey as a Babe in His Mother's arms.

Being in the Temple at the ritual of libation, He raised His voice and exclaimed: "If any man thirst, let him come, and I will give him to drink of living water" (see John 7:37–38). When, again, He thought of the seven-branched candlestick, set above its massive stand to illuminate the Temple, He cried out: "I am the Light of the world" (see John 8:12; 9:5). And His heart, yearning for souls, while watching the sheep being driven in from the desert to Judea for the sacrifice, burst forth in glowing words: "I am the Door; no one goes to the Father but by me" (see John 10:9). And all the people cried out with one voice: 'No man hath ever spoken like this man!' And they forgot all things while listening to His word: "And the crowds were in admiration of Him" (see Matt. 7:28–29).

When He asked them, "Have you understood all these things?" they answered, "Yea, yea!" (see Matt. 13:51). And then, casting a net, as it were, over all He had said, He concluded in that phrase, simple as Nature herself yet deep as the Infinite: "Amen, Amen, I say to you: this generation shall not pass till all these things be accomplished. Heaven and earth shall pass away, but my words shall never pass away" (Mark 13:30–31).

Oh, what an awful truth lies behind the simple splendor of these divine words! What a vision rises before us! What terrible images! How they echo — those words of power — in one single sound through myriads of ages! Who can tell the mysterious history of the stars — vain evolutions, terrific cataclysms, worlds crumbling to nothingness, which God can change, as the psalmist says, as men change their cloaks (see Ps. 101:27 [102:26])? And His word remains, unchanged, unchangeable, in the midst of the wreck and ruin of worlds, suffering no taint or destruction, and living eternally, the one sublime law for all.

∞

As to the *authority* of our Divine Master's word, we need not say much, for we well know whence it came. "His words were full of power," we are told in the Gospel. "He spoke as one having authority, and not like the scribes" (see Matt. 7:29). Indeed, He was the first, the only One, who of Himself had divine authority to teach.

For who has power and right to teach man? Truth, and Truth alone. He who is not truth and rests on his own authority deceives himself and deceives his hearers. But Jesus Christ *is* Truth; He is Truth incarnate. This is why He does not quote or refer to anyone. He speaks, and He demands that we believe His word. He taught His disciples as God taught the first man Adam—with a calmness that proceeded from His own consciousness of truth and inspired this sentiment in others.

We need not discuss it. "Amen, Amen, *I* say to thee" (see, e.g., Matt. 5:18). Is this not enough for us, we who know who it is that speaks? His calm certitude establishes His doctrine beyond all human discussion; in the inaccessible regions of eternity, and under the form of an aphorism or a parable, or in one short, clear sentence that enlightens the mind, He opposes all error, explains the most knotty problems, defeats the shrewdest sophistry, and breaks to fragments the most wily arguments, as a stone thrown among glass shivers it to atoms. His enemies are reduced to silence, while the multitudes cry out: "Bene dixisti, Magister!" ("Master, Thou hast spoken well!"; see Mark 12:32). And no man dared ask Him any more questions.

Truly, He who spoke was no ordinary orator. He had within Him the certitude of God; He had also the power of God. He could seal every word He spoke with a miracle had He so willed, and could have called on the powers of Heaven to bear witness to His truth.

He had also, *humanly* speaking, all the characteristics that showed forth His truth. He had disinterestedness, His only solicitude being for His Father's glory. He had true love for His people. While others flattered and betrayed them, He corrected, consoled, and cured, like a kind and loving father. Added to this, He had a charm comprising all ideal grace and noble attractions; and, above all, His was the ideally pure life, spent in doing good to all, of a perfection hitherto unknown to men. When His enemies would resist His doctrine, He turned to them, and said: "Which of you can convince me of sin?" and their guilty silence gave the answer. Did this not give Him the right to add: "Why will you not believe in Me?" (John 8:46). His life answered for His doctrine and made all shadow of error or deceit an impossibility. He was holy, Holiness itself, and He was true, Truth itself, for these cannot be separated. Oh, blessed days that heard the sound of His words! Oh, blessed places that gathered their fragrance as they fell!

Today, when we visit these hallowed spots, so silent, so sad, these memories crowd around us. Everything we see recalls some event in His life or one of His parables, and we advance with respect and loving awe as in a temple, or as advancing up an avenue of triumph. This land where Jesus lived, these skies that hung above His head, these hills that echoed to His voice, these earthly objects by which He used to teach eternal truths, all stir our souls and plunge them into an ecstasy of love, while they invite us again and again to read His Gospels.

Why do we read them so little?

Chapter 4

∞

The Prayer of Jesus

※

In speaking of Nazareth, we have already said that the *exterior* life and work of our Divine Savior was only secondary. His primary work was a hidden work, consisting of His communion with God His Father and with the souls of men.

This fact need not surprise us, for we often feel the same to be the case with regard to ourselves. Can men judge us merely by our words or actions? The surface of our life — what those around us can see — is like a light crust, beneath which lies our soul, all that interior world of thoughts, desires, tendencies, aspirations, dreams, joys, and sorrows — all, indeed, that makes us what we are. In order that we may be known, we must not be judged by our words only, but also by our silence; not by our actions alone, but also by our repose. In short, we are truly understood by the *interior* life we live, half hiddenly, which appears but dimly among the activities that are seen on the surface, even as a world of living creatures live and flourish in the depths of the sea far beneath its calm or stormy waves.

In Jesus Christ this truth is infinitely profound. But then, you may ask, what does it signify where His public life was spent, or how long it lasted, if His real life was lived within Himself, *alone*? But we know this was not the case.

He acted in all things outwardly for our instruction, but it was essentially within His soul that His great work was effected. There between Him and His Heavenly Father was the great act accomplished. We can see this in considering the prayer of Jesus.

That Jesus prayed there can be no doubt, for the Gospel repeatedly affirms it. What we will consider is the explanation of this act on the part of Jesus, for at first sight it may appear a contradiction.

Jesus is God. Can we dare to say that, as God, He ever prayed? But He is also man, and as man He is so closely united to the Divinity that we cannot imagine what prayer could add to Him, or what it could accomplish for Him who had no imperfection to draw His soul from its celestial heights. Nevertheless, the will of Jesus, inasmuch as it resembles ours—which at times longs for a desired object—could seek and at times even be restless to be alone with God in prayer.

It was necessary for Jesus to demonstrate the close tie that existed between His Father and Him, and nothing could show this more effectually than the intimate union of His prayer and its unfailing success. Likewise our Divine Savior wished to give us an example. He obeyed, although He need not have obeyed; suffered, although He need not have suffered; died, although He need not have died; and in like manner He prayed to give us an example, in order that, like Him, we might "pray always" (see Luke 18:1).

In the first place, it is clear that Jesus prayed according to the conditions laid down by the Jewish law: in the synagogue, as we have said, and in the Temple, where the worship of God, so scrupulously observed, comprised a great number of vocal prayers. Notably, each evening, at the end of the day's devotions, the service of libation was performed, during which the Levites intoned the psalms, accompanied by the music of the Temple. Each psalm was divided into three sections; at each interval, the priests sounded their silver trumpets three times as a signal for the people to adore. Nothing was omitted that could add dignity to the ceremony. The worshipper was required to bow gradually, solemnly, and in silence. He must hold in his hand neither staff nor sandals, neither purse nor bag. It would seem that these same exhortations addressed by our Divine Master to His disciples at the close of His ministry, when He sent them to preach, were given them in order to remind them that their apostolate was to be a worship in every way as perfect as that according to the old Law in the Temple (see Mark 6:8).

The posture of the Jew during prayer was with the head inclined, the knees sometimes bent, at other times the body prostrate, as our Savior Himself prayed during His agony in the garden. When standing upright the worshipper was to have his mantle folded about him, his feet together, his eyes cast to the ground, his hands resting on his breast; in short, as we are told by the Doctors of the Church, he must stand before God "as a servant before his master, in all reverence and fear."

We can picture our Divine Master, modest and grave, praying in accents of love in His Father's house. He observed the Jewish worship before abolishing it. He offered the last grains of incense before destroying the altar.

In the second place, Jesus prayed with His Apostles. He said: "Wheresoever two or three are gathered in my name, I am in the midst of them" (see Matt. 18:20); and we cannot doubt that this saying of His was often carried out to the letter.

Sometimes, with the Apostles grouped around Him, some-times with two or three chosen ones, as on Tabor, He showed them how to pray, and animated them by His example. One day in particular, He taught them this lesson with a grand and special solemnity. It was on the Mount of Olives. After the turmoil of the day, passed in the Temple disputing with the Doctors, Jesus retired apart with His disciples. Beneath the lofty dome of in-terlacing leaves He sought a retreat, and St. Luke tells us that here He often passed the night.

Wearily the little band climbed the hill after the heat and toil of the day, and reaching the summit, the disciples paused and, turning to Jesus, said: "Master, teach us to pray" (Luke 11:1).

Standing in their midst, with the holy city lying spread out as a panorama behind Him, while, at the foot of the hill beyond the Kedron, the Temple rose in its calm splendor — a reflection of the solitary majesty of God — Jesus gave to them and to all the world that sublime lesson of prayer: "When you pray, pray thus: Our Father, who art in Heaven, hallowed be Thy name. Thy kingdom come. Thy will be done on earth as it is in Heaven. Give us this day our daily bread, and forgive us our trespasses, as we forgive them that trespass against us. And lead us not into temptation, but deliver us from evil."

In modern times, on the spot that tradition has handed down as being the place where that first Our Father was spoken, a pious princess has raised a monument of faith and love. She caused a chapel to be erected, around which a cloister runs, and in the walls of this cloister are set marble tablets, each bearing in one of thirty-two languages the words of the Our Father.[1] Thus does

---

[1] Aurélie de Bossi, the princess de la Tour d'Auvergne, the Italian widow of a French prince, had a devotion to the Our Father.

the whole world repeat in all tongues and at all times the ideal petitions that came to earth directly from Heaven.

But most often Jesus prayed alone, and it is this form of His prayer that we will consider more closely—first, as to its *exterior conditions*, and secondly, as far as is possible to us, as to its *matter*.

Apart from the prayers in the Temple and in the synagogue, every Jew, according to the rabbinical rule, was directed to pray three times a day, and we cannot doubt that in this respect, as in all else, our Savior submitted to the law.

We can imagine that at night, free from all earthly fetters, this prayer was much prolonged. He may have given His body rest—necessary repose—but this was doubtless of very short duration.

The sleep of Jesus was not like our sleep—caused by weariness of body overcoming the mind, the earth, as it were, showing its claim on us, and we powerless to resist it. His sleep was the rest He willingly gave Himself; His soul—supreme mistress of His body—regulated its measure and form, and never for a moment did He lose selfconsciousness.

May we not reverently conjecture that after having all day acted, preached, worked, suffered, borne His earthly life—laborious and humble—when night came, and the world was wrapped in sleep, Jesus entered entirely—body and soul—into the beatific repose of infinity. The day He spent on earth; at night He raised Himself to Heaven.

The present church, called the Pater Noster Church, and its cloister were completed in 1874. "Church of Pater Noster," SeeTheHolyLand.net, https://www.seetheholyland.net/church-of-pater-noster/. —Ed.

This raising of His soul had its symbol in His outward action. Jesus loved to pray on the mountains. "He retired into the mountain Himself alone"; "He went to the mountain to pray" (see Matt. 14:23; Mark 6:46). The ancient prophets also prayed thus. From earliest times the "high places," as they are called in the Bible, were looked upon as places specially set apart for souls desiring secret commune with God, and it was thus that Jesus loved to pray.

At the quiet evening hour, when Heaven itself seemed to slumber, drawing its light away from earth, and the proud sun lay silent and unseen, Jesus left His faithful followers. He climbed some lonely slope alone. Leaving below Him the earth, with its smile of fading day, shaking from Him the dust of earthly waysides, He rose and went to the region of the stars; and there, invaded with the peace from on high, His soul laid itself open to the ecstasy of Heaven. Like a chalice, wherein the consecrated species reposes, and which the priest raises in his hands to offer to the Sovereign Lord of all things, so was the humanity of Jesus at this silent evening hour.

He left below Him, He forgot (if we may so speak) all human things, all visible objects connected with His great work and entered entirely into the infinite abyss of the ineffable majesty of God. There He held converse with the Father—converse that it is not given to man to conceive. Mysterious dialogue between God and God! Infinity and Immensity, between the Creator and Him who became a creature. How can we attempt to penetrate into the awful silence of that prayer?

In the bosom of the night, which magnifies all things—night, which is so vast, which seems to raise earthly objects and clothe them with mystery, and which is, says Denis the Areopagite, "the most faithful image of God"—Jesus entered into the vast realms of infinity.

This little earth was no longer anything to Him. His soul sailed on the seas of infinite space and shone with an ineffable grandeur twofold divine, a grandeur that man's eye might not behold. As God, He was Principal of all; as man, burdened with all, giving life to all, leading souls in mysterious paths, being at once God and man, doing the work of God and the work of Christ. He bestowed, yet He petitioned; He offered sacrifice, and yet He received the universal offerings of creation.

And all the while the little planet revolved at His feet, ignorant of whom it bore; and the stars, pursuing their nightly course, looked on Him as faithful servants watching their Master. They hovered around the spot where their incarnate Lord reposed, making a glory over His earthly resting place. Let us now seek to draw nearer and consider more closely the matter of the prayer of Jesus.

We cannot pretend to penetrate its mystery or fathom its depth, for this is the privilege of those who are borne away in ecstasies of divine love, such as St. Paul, who was raised to the third heaven (2 Cor. 12:2), or St. John, who gazed on Divinity with the clear, strong glance of the eagle — these giants who, while living still on earth, could pierce the heavens. Like the high mountains, whose feet are planted in the valleys and whose summits are lost in the clouds far out of sight, these saints might have told us something of the prayer of Jesus, but they have been careful to withhold from us those things that it is not permitted to man to utter. Yet we will try to speak of these mysteries, try to analyze, in our poor human way, the prayer of the Master — so that knowledge may lead to greater love. To what human qualities do His sentiments correspond? What transports of soul do they inspire?

The first human quality is doubtless adoration. Adoration is the first act of justice that God demands. God is. When He shows

Himself, He proves His rights, because He is the one essential Being. His existence is absolute, without limitation, unchangeable, and necessary. As the apex or center of a million rays, His being sheds itself in all His attributes. Intelligence, will, love, goodness, fecundity, justice, power — the list prolonged to infinity, and each perfection extended to its utmost plenitude, and all in perfect union, in absolute simplicity, and incomprehensible eternity; this is God. All other beings who possess any reflection of these perfections possess them only through Him, possess them in Him; and as it is possible for Him to take these gifts from them, He is more master of them than are the creatures themselves, so that it is but justice for them to acknowledge that they have nothing and that He possesses all things.

To adore is to acknowledge the *all* of the person adored and the *nothingness* of him who adores. It is to proclaim that the person adored has all perfections, all rights, all being.

Adoration is nothingness fainting and willingly expiring in self-annihilation before the face of the Infinite. This is what Jesus did.

He acknowledged that a creature is nothing but a breath from the divine mouth. He recognized that even He was nothing, in terms of the wonderful humanity to which He was hypostatically united. "Why dost thou call me good?" He said one day to the young man who had called Him good. "None is good, but God alone" (see Luke 18:19). One only is great, and the human Christ, with all His glory, was only a ray of God. So Jesus, by His supreme act of adoration, mounted reverently to His own Source. Rapt in the intoxicating calm of the Eastern night, under the scintillation of the stars — now fading away, now glowing ardently like coals of fire — or in the pale light of the cold white moon, the humanity of Jesus lost itself in sublime adoration, drawing within itself all creation, that all alike might worship God. That wonderful force that we call Nature, its music, painting, noble architecture — all were present when He made that act; all joined in proclaiming the glory of God, and the heart of Jesus beat in harmony with His creatures. For He who was as a great universe holding within Him all creation offered Himself to Heaven as the representative of all things made. Thus was the world once more restored to God; and the soul of Jesus, bearing by its union with the Word an infinite power, rendered to God, for the first time since the world was made, the greatest act of justice, God being adored as He ought to be adored.

As a consequence of these rights that Jesus Christ acknowledged to His Father — sovereign rights, which implied sovereign dominion — He abandoned into His Father's hands His life — His individual life and the life of His work.

His Father had a plan; it was Jesus' duty to carry it out. Thus, during His nightly repose He arranged the work of the day; He regulated each detail in intimate union with His Father. He saw before Him His field of battle, His field of work, the field of His death, which was, in reality, the field of His triumph; and His loving heart following His vision, He, in advance, accepted *all*, obeying "even unto death" (see Phil. 2:8).

And what of the future life of His work? In what way did He regard that? What did He say concerning it in His silent converse with God? How much importance did He attach to it in His prayer? This was perhaps the greatest mystery in the life of Christ. Terrible to contemplate! The work of Jesus upon earth must be, apparently, unworthy of Him — apparently, a failure.

He had come to raise up the world, to deliver it from the tyranny of evil, to restore it to God. He said this Himself, and the vehement expressions He made use of show the extreme ardor of

His desires. "I am come to cast fire upon the earth, and what will I but that it be enkindled?" (Luke 12:49). But the earth was as ice to His touch. His immediate work met with nothing but rebuffs.

His first ministry at Nazareth ended in a rebuff: they wanted to cast Him down from the mountain. His preaching in Galilee met with rebuffs: He terminated it with a malediction. His death was again another, and, to the eyes of men, the greatest, rebuff; and one of the words He uttered on the Cross, "*Consummatum est*" (It is finished; see John 19:30), sounds like the last sigh of a broken heart, the farewell to a fallen hope.

To believe this—namely, that Christ's work on earth was a failure—would be a blasphemy; but what we *may* say is this: that during His life He only sowed the seed. He said: "The kingdom of Heaven is like unto a mustard seed, the smallest of all seeds," but He tells us that it is the seed of a great tree, and that great tree did not rise till after many years had passed (see Mark 4:31–32). How slowly, how laboriously, and after how many vicissitudes and troubled experiences! Search history, and what do you find? They say that the Gospel is no more than smoke that has passed away and left no trace. This is false, absolutely false! The grain *has* brought forth its fruit, but "in patience," as our Savior foretold (see Luke 8:15).

Read St. Paul's Epistles! Listen to his laments. See him panting from his labors, overcoming his fears. Behold the little churches that rose slowly, humbly, and then, as they grew, divided again to form other churches.

And, later, see! Surely there were triumphs, miraculous triumphs, for God's cause. *Miraculous* is the only word suitable, and yet, though they were so miraculous from a human point of view, how little they were in comparison with the desires of Christ!

The desires of Christ! That burning furnace of love! That torrent of fire, which numberless oceans could not extinguish! What has it found on earth that can ever satisfy its flames?

The ideal reign of God, for which Jesus longed with all the power of His being, will never be perfected on earth. Never will God's will "be done on earth as it is in Heaven." That stupendous prayer, that petition of fire, that supplication, comprising all perfections, that we call the Our Father, must ever be for man a simple, grand ideal toward which he strives, but which can never be attained on earth.

And Jesus, the Christ, the Ideal Man, must resign Himself that this should be so. All that He could do was to make up to God, by the gift of Himself, the shortcomings of His creatures: to supply by His own life for that which they are not; by His own power for that which they cannot do; by the gift of Himself for that which they will not give. This was his role, and when He prolonged His prayer far into the night, it was because He would cast into the bosom of His Father the superabundance of His soul, thus atoning for the ingratitude of men.

But the prayer of Jesus was not made only to atone for the small harvest that His labors would yield in the future. It also had relation to the fruitful, if tardy, results of His ministry. True, it would require centuries — many centuries — of strife to complete the divine edifice; and upon how many ruins must it not be built! on what mountains of defeat! God is, in truth, a strange Workman; His methods are disconcerting to human reason, for there is no shade of hurry or anxiety in His work. What are a few centuries to Him who can increase them to infinity? We see this in God's method of creating the earth. After what terrible and numberless states of transformation did He call forth form out of chaos, and life out of nothingness! And, again, from the first trembling vibration of life in the depths of the sea, who can tell what myriads of centuries elapsed before man came to claim the earth, as a reaper gathering the ripe harvest?

Again, glancing at the history of man, how slow, how tedious is the march of civilization—from the shepherd races, wandering tribes, and barbarous nations, to the great Eastern civilization, the proud days of the Roman Empire, with its pomp and wild display, leading up gradually to our day, which will fade and wander from us into the unknown paths of the future. All this is the work of God, who rules and regulates all time, and, consequently, it is the work of Christ, for God gave the earth to His Christ, and He sent His Holy Spirit to renew the face of the earth.

What delays! What pauses! What shocks! What recoils! And if, as we see, God makes no haste in His work, why should Christ, the word of God, be anxious or perturbed that His Father's honor was so slowly recognized and worshipped? He, to whom all past and future were present in His prayer, sighed with patient yearning, and was consumed with ardent desire for God's kingdom upon earth; and as His will was in all things resigned to His Father's will, may we not affirm that He offered all His heartfelt longing to God as an earnest of future reality?

Such was the primary object of the intimate prayer of Jesus. He adored His Father, and desired with an intense longing for God's glory. And, as a consequence of this desire, did He not ask anything for man? Had He no petitions to make for man? Oh, can we doubt that in His prayer Jesus remembered His friends? One day He said to Simon Peter: "Simon, Simon, Satan hath desired to sift you as wheat; but *I have prayed for thee*, that thy faith fail not" (Luke 22:31–32).

Certainly, Simon was not the only one to benefit by our Savior's prayers. He united all His loved ones in His heart—all

His own, both present and future—and so He prayed for *us*. It would be blasphemy for any one of us to say: "He did not pray for us; we did not come before His mind; and it was not for each of us that His heart throbbed and burned." What did He ask of the Father for us? All! all! not even forgetting that simple need for bread that we poor human creatures must ever remember. He foresaw that continual want; He had pity on us, and *He* said for us, that we might say it after Him: "Father, give us this day our daily bread."

But it was in a special manner for our spiritual needs that He prayed. He made us and He knew us; therefore, He knew what to ask for us.

We are sinful and weak. Because we are sinful, He begged for our forgiveness. Because we are weak, He asked for—what? That temptation might not touch us? That evil might not approach? That the enemy should not assail us? No. Jesus prayed for none of these things. He knew that it would not be well for us if difficulties did not arise. It is in adversity, not in security and idleness, that the soul grows strong. If a general would prove the valor and fidelity of a soldier, will he leave him behind in safety to look after the food or the baggage? Does he not rather put him in the battlefield, in the hope that victory crown his efforts?

Such also is Jesus. He does not expect His soldiers *always* to gain the victory in every encounter, but as He "desires not the death of the sinner" (see Ezek. 18:32), He prayed that all might ultimately conquer. Although He prayed that His own might be faithful, He did not pray that they might never fall, because He knew our poor nature and the daily difficulties of human life.

Jesus knew that oftentimes our greatest virtues have their root in our miseries and defeats. He who gazed down into the most secret chambers of our souls, and to whom the most hidden thoughts were bright as day, saw clearly by which path each and every soul must travel to its goal. The road must always be one of struggle and temptation. We would not dare speak thus if great saints and Doctors had not spoken so before us; but many have told us so after bitter personal experiences. Was it not St. Augustine, a man whose authority cannot be questioned, who pronounced those bold words: "For those who love God all turns to good, even their sins"? *Etiam peccata!* Conflict is necessary, we may say; so also is defeat! Jesus Christ allowed His Apostles to be defeated. He called Simon "Cephas," "a rock," and said to him: "I have prayed for thee that thy faith fail not"; and yet He permitted him to fall three times, and that most shamefully. Peter kept the faith — that is to say, his conviction in Jesus. He retained his confidence, his attachment, his desire of good, and the love that was buried deep in his heart below his weakness; but he fell, and Jesus permitted it. Why? Because He knew that in the supernatural edifice, the groundwork and foundation is not strength, but *humility*, and humility is a pearl that can only be dug out of the dust of defeat. We must realize that we have the weakness within us before we can look outside for the remedy to strengthen us. And Jesus well knew when He allowed Simon Peter to fall that the future love of that Apostle would feed on this memory as its best nourishment, and that this remembrance, bitter and never buried, as we know it to have been, would goad him on in his labors, even to his martyrdom, as a spur ever tearing the sides of a horse that bears its rider through the thick of the fight.

After the Resurrection, Jesus one day turned to Peter, and said: "Peter, lovest thou me?" Peter answered: "Lord, Thou knowest that I love Thee!" Again: "Peter, lovest thou me?" "Lord, Thou knowest that I love Thee." And yet again: "Peter, lovest thou Me?" A flood of tears gushed from the eyes of Peter. He understood; it was his triple denial that the kind Master would wipe out. Oh, that memory! How it burned and cut his soul and inundated it with grief! Yes, but also it opened the sluices of his love, and showed the firm foundation of the future Church of Christ; for when the Savior had finished His questioning, and Simon had thrice protested his love, Jesus said: "Feed my lambs, feed my sheep" (John 21:15–17); and the penitent was given all power of pardon and authority. Peter's feet were planted in Rome, where the cross of martyrdom awaited him.

In our temptations and our troubles, let us remember the prayer of Jesus; let us join our prayer to His, and pray as He prayed, that our prayers may be heard, and we may grow strong in His strength.

For us, as for Jesus, to pray is to go to the mountaintop, to seek strength and peace at its Source — the Source of life and of rest. It is, at one and the same time, to fortify and to defend ourselves, to hide ourselves under the armor of God, to sharpen our weapons for the fight; it is to realize that we are nothing, but that with God we can do all things. And when we have done this, we need have no fear: God in Heaven will do the rest.

One day, when Jesus was constrained to withdraw Himself from the passionate enthusiasm of the people, who would seize Him to make Him king, He fled for refuge, according to His custom, to the mountain. Again, another day, while He prayed on the hilltop, He saw His disciples from afar struggling with the waves in the stormy lake below. It was one of those sudden tempests so prevalent on the Sea of Galilee, which in a few moments become raging storms, and no doubt the disciples, in their danger, turned their thoughts to their Master. Jesus, powerful and kind, His prayer finished, used His power, and, without delay or hesitation, went to His children's aid, walking on the water. How often Jesus acts thus with His faithful ones! After He has prayed for us, He comes. He walks on the sea of adversity, which is our life—or that other tempestuous ocean, our soul—and all is calm.

He says: "It is I: fear not," as He said in the Gospel (Matt. 14:27), and softly our boat comes safety to the shore. The shore for which we long is peace; it is safety after trouble and defeat; it is the beginning again after misery and failure.

Again, the shore to which we are journeying is Heaven. Oh, Heaven, boundary of earth's struggles, harbor of peace in the joys of reward, eternal goal toward which Jesus directs our vessel with the gentle breath of His prayer, and where, with Jesus, the just will find eternal rest.

Chapter 5

∞

Jesus and the Jewish Authority

∞

In his Epistle to the Romans, St. Paul pronounces those words so often quoted but so seldom acted upon, either by those who govern or those who obey: "There is no power but from God" (13:1). Even the authority that some men exercise over others that has its origin in either a contract, willingly consented to, or in the power of strength over weakness — even this authority comes from God; because, in reality, no man has a right to govern another. We are free, and everything that Nature or circumstances may confer on such or such a superior establishes in itself no authority over the person of another. What is it, then, that permits one man, or a group of men, to govern? It can only be called a species of delegation, which has God for its first principle.

God made man a social being, and as the social body cannot exist without some bond or authority, he on whom this authority is bestowed exercises it by God, and so it is in reality to Him that we render our homage. This being so, Jesus, as the Ideal and Perfect Man, would not dispense Himself from respecting authority, and insofar as was compatible with His designs, He submitted to it. Not that He owed obedience to any man, but He was the example for all to imitate; and it is needless to say that in this, as in every other respect, He set the example for us to follow.

As a private individual, if we may use the term, He obeyed the laws of His nation in every respect. Willingly He submitted to the circumcision, He observed the Sabbath, He paid the tribute, He frequented the synagogue, He went to Jerusalem regularly for the appointed feast days.

In His public actions we find Him equally, if not more, respectful to authority on account of the grave consequences to His disciples that must necessarily follow on His actions. In His day, work was the rule; in fact, it was looked upon almost as a necessity, not only because it was an old institution that all should work, but also in order to bring calm and peace to the spirit.

The Jewish nation was in a state of turmoil, and profoundly troubled. Incapable of bearing patiently the Roman yoke, which seemed to them a profanation, they broke out periodically into revolts of a fury verging on madness. Riots frequently took place; they were smothered in streams of blood; but, as is always the case, bloodshed thus served only to irrigate the roots of their hatred and made it grow stronger and more unquenchable than ever. Two thousand insurgents had been crucified at the gate of the city after one of these revolts. A frightful sight, which made those whose ardent patriotism had earned for them the name of *zealots* writhe with anger. The result of this action was that, instead of quelling the rebels, a sort of terrible enthusiasm was aroused in their fierce souls, as was a longing for revenge and a thirst for the blood of their Roman rulers.

Besides all this public strife, there were internal dissensions, rivalries of sects, struggles for influence, jealousies, burning controversies, suspicious plots, civil wars among citizens.

If Jesus loved His country, He must, then, act in a manner to strengthen the bonds that, while holding all power outside the authority of the law, could arm itself for the common good.

In times of trouble and dissensions, when all the energies of the nation are sapped and exhausted, leaving the people like a worthless corpse, ready for corruption, then the duty of a real patriot is plain. He must gather the people around him and animate them with his spirit of honesty — not quarrel with them on the pretext of political opposition, nor show any personal preference. The common safety is in danger, and the remedy can come only from unity of action; and that action, in order to be efficacious, must be permeated with a spirit of submission and obedience.

Jesus loved His country. That feeling so strong in every human heart, which is partly instinctive and partly deliberate, called patriotism, was not unfamiliar to Him, only in Him it was higher and more perfect than it is in us. Instead of that element of weakness with which patriotism, sacred as it is in itself, is so often accompanied; instead of that almost sentimental idea with which we regard our native place — as a sort of refuge for us from the wild tempest of trouble, as a child runs for shelter to his mother's arms — instead of these all-too-human sentiments, the patriotism of Jesus was grand and strong and perfect. He loved His country and His people, and His loyalty to them exceeded infinitely all our conceptions of love of country, even as an atom is lost in infinity.

He had, as man, a special predilection for that land in which it was His Father's will that He should be born. And yet we read in the Gospel that Jesus constantly opposed Jewish authority. When He went to Jerusalem for the great feasts, He was in perpetual conflict with the rulers. Why was this so?

It was because, however respectful our Divine Lord might be to authority, and however desirous of maintaining peace, He could not resign His authority, nor could He ignore the work He had come to do. Respect for earthly power has its limitations;

in excess, it serves to destroy rather than to edify. Jesus came on earth to edify and to establish a spiritual power. If, then, He found any resistance, there was but one thing for Him to do: break the opposing force, and, above all things, guard that which was essential to His work—namely, His liberty.

This, then, is what we must understand when we consider the relations of Jesus with the Jewish authorities. There is, indeed, a false liberty that consists in judging without the right to judge, in seizing without permission, in condemning without authority; but we cannot speak of this sort of liberty in connection with Him who possessed all rights and authority and who was the Source of all wisdom. His conduct was always prudent, and well did He demonstrate to all that He was master of His work, His actions, and Himself. We will glance at one little episode that shows this forth most clearly. St. Luke reports the incident.

Jesus was in Galilee, which was then under the jurisdiction of Herod. While He was preaching before a great crowd of people, the Pharisees, pretending to be anxious as to His personal safety, came to Him and said: "Depart, and get Thee hence, for Herod hath a mind to kill Thee." He answered: "Go and tell that fox, Behold I cast out devils, and do cures today and tomorrow, and the third day I am consummated. Nevertheless, I must walk today and tomorrow, and the day following, because it cannot be that a prophet perish out of Jerusalem" (Luke 13:31–33). What wonderful words! What tranquil majesty they hold! What grave simplicity they bear! Does He not here show all that He is free? Is He not in very truth a Master?

"Go, tell that fox!" He calls him by his name, this crowned impostor, coward and murderer. What an example He sets for those who, in moments of weakness and tepidity, though they have the right to speak—indeed, whose duty it is to speak—think they can serve God by maintaining a cowardly silence.

He will not allow His truth to resign its rights to those who, even on the pretext of prudence or charity, try to silence the representatives of Christ. As though we could be prudent only by being cowardly! As if truth could be preserved only by being hidden under a bushel! As though one could show love for one's brother by abandoning him to the treachery and snares of his enemies!

And what message did He send to this "fox," Herod? He said: "Behold, I cast out devils, and do cures today and tomorrow; after that is the hour of the powers of darkness. I will suffer all that I must suffer, and meanwhile, I will accomplish that which I have come to do. After three days will come my death, but death *because* I will it, and *where* I will it—not in your kingdom, O ruler of Galilee, but in Jerusalem. 'It cannot be that a prophet perish out of Jerusalem.' A soldier must die on the battlefield, a workman at his work, a shepherd amidst his flock—a prophet must die at Jerusalem. Meanwhile, I labor and do my appointed task. Today, tomorrow, the day following are mine. I accomplish my designs in spite of *you*; if necessary, I will act in defiance of you. I have no fear, and I will not allow you to hinder me by fetter or snare."

Such is the attitude of Jesus before man's authority—no provocation, but absolute liberty.

Jesus was not often called upon to maintain His liberty with regard to Herod. It was only at the close of His life, and then merely in passing, that He asserted His rights and showed His power over this prince. But with the Jewish authority it was quite another thing. Jesus took His stand on religious grounds, and in Jerusalem, religion and political power, church and state, were one and the same thing; consequently, the Sanhedrin, the high priests, the Pharisees, and the scribes all rose up and opposed Him. Which must give way? That was the question. Jesus would not, could not, change one detail of His great work. They must accept *His* authority, acknowledge it, and conform to it. Did they do this? We know the answer well, but it will not be without fruit for us to contemplate the subject more closely.

How many sublime lessons are hidden in the conduct of Jesus toward the great ones of this world!

In His dealings with men Jesus had two forces to contend with, which were always rising in all their strength to oppose His work. These were (1) the past, with its customs, and (2) the passions of men.

The past is a force; it is the root whence we have sprung, and the longer the root has been planted, the harder it is to uproot. We have, it is true, within us the instinct of the Eternal, of a definite end to be attained; it is a sign of our destiny. But this instinct frequently becomes weakened and dormant, because it is difficult to detach ourselves sufficiently from that which is always before us, and thus we easily become narrow and selfish.

The past is of our own making; it is ourselves in a certain sense that we recall in it, and it is the past that repeats itself again and again in the blind struggle of life.

It is hard to escape from the past; to do so, it would be necessary to lose sight of oneself, to detach oneself from one's natural surroundings, and to keep in sight only the aspirations of the future. This few can do.

To overcome the past, one must possess either genius or sanctity, and one is as rare as the other. Like the great wave that rises o'er the billow, with foaming crest, and sinks again out of sight, so is genius: rearing a moment with proud, strong head, then falling forgotten in the ocean of time. Most men follow the ordinary routine of mediocrity; they are content with the already formed opinions of other men—the established laws—and they follow in deeply furrowed grooves cut out by the customs of the past. New ideas make them uneasy; hardship and struggle frighten them; they prefer to look to the past than to gaze at the future; and since they are content to build for themselves houses of clay out of the past that no longer lives, it is but natural that these representatives of a dead and bygone day should rebel against new ideas and oppose all innovations.

Jesus was an initiator, even to an alarming degree. He found on earth Judaism, the inspired religion of God; but this religion was ordained by God only to be a precursor of His Church, and consequently, when Christ came, it no longer had any reason for existing. Thus, Jesus the Messiah came, and it was the flame of His word that burned up, as it were, the dry wood of the Old Testament.

Was not this in itself sufficient to render Him worthy of the suspicion even of those who, in good faith, were following the doctrines of their fathers?

It is difficult for us to realize to what an extent Jesus had to overthrow the old Jewish religion. Imbued as we are with Christian principles, which have governed the human mind for centuries past, we cannot fathom what novelties these very principles must have seemed in the days when Jesus promulgated them on the Lake of Galilee. Jesus did not present Himself or His doctrine to the people without laying claim to certain rights and titles, nor could those whom He condemned be excused on the plea of ignorance. "If I had not come and spoken to them, they would not have sin; but now they have no excuse for their sin. He that hateth me hateth my Father also" (John 15:22–23).

The crime of the Jews was not that they found the doctrine of Jesus strange, or that they were scandalized by it; it was that they would not acknowledge our Savior's titles and right to teach and that they persisted in condemning Him as an impostor and a seducer of the people. They always had some pretext for opposing Him, and they ever managed to color their opposition with a semblance of truth.

We well know in what emphatic terms Jesus proposed His doctrine: "Moses said unto you, 'Do *this*'; I say, 'Do *that*.' Moses commanded *this*; I command *that*." Think of it! To speak thus to the Jews. To stand up against Moses and reform his laws. It was sacrilege, it was treason; because to the Jews, Moses was people and religion and law; no one could touch Moses without, at one and the same time, overturning all these.

Jesus announced the ruin of the Temple, the Temple so dear to them all, which was in truth the home and center of the people, the religion, and the law. He attacked and condemned the priests, who were the leaders of the people and taught religion and the law.

He spoke kindly to the Gentiles, and announced their incorporation in His Church. The Jewish exclusiveness was fifteen centuries old and had been established by God Himself; and if now Jesus would have them believe that the time for it was past, and that in the days to come there must be no distinction between Jew or pagan, Greek or barbarian, but that all humanity must profess one creed, then truly His was a doctrine hard to believe, and their cold and narrow hearts would not open to it. And then to this hardness and narrowness the priests and rulers in Jerusalem added passion, hypocrisy, and vice.

These were the men whom Jesus opposed. We may ask how it was that Jesus, gentleness itself, appeared so severe to the priests and doctors of the law. This is a question that often confronts us, and it lays bare a very common delusion.

There are some who would always like to picture Jesus as the meek "Lamb of God"; the One who was "meek and humble of heart"; the Man who spoke sweet parables and gave gentle discourses; the fair Boy so often painted in pious pictures, with sunny locks and soft white hands, mild even to effeminacy. No, Jesus Christ was not at all times like that. He was meek and humble of heart above all, but when occasion arose, He was terrible also. He shows us God in every form, if we may dare so to speak, and from His own words we learn two facts about His character: God is our Father, and so tenderly does He love us that even the very hairs of our head are numbered; but, also, God is He of whom it is said: "It is awful to fall into the hands of the living God" (see Heb. 10:31). Great as is His mercy toward the repentant sinner, and deep as is His compassion for His weakest child, so great and so deep is also His anger against the proud and the false of heart.

We will give a cursory glance at those men who were in authority when Jesus was on earth, and then we will understand why He spoke to them so severely.

There were two powers in Jerusalem opposed to our Divine Lord, and both were equally strong: the priests and the men of science. The first body of men were composed chiefly of the Sadducees, comprising the high priest and the scribes. These were called the

Sanhedrin, an assembly that was at the same time a tribunal, a parliament, and a council. These men, while calling themselves Sadducees — that is, "just men" — were in reality men of money and of intrigue. They trafficked in piety and yet did not practice it. St. Paul tells us that it is the right of the priest to "live by the altar" (see 1 Cor. 9:13), but woe to that priest who *lives* by the altar but does not *work* for the altar.

The Sadducees were content with an official piety. An odious combination of pride and baseness, of brutality and astuteness, of tyranny and servility, they oppressed the people, crushed them beneath their pomp and haughtiness, and then turned to cringe and grovel at the feet of the Romans.

They were "preservers" or "keepers," it is true, but this title, so honorable in itself, they used as a cloak for their treachery and cruelty. Estimable as is he who preserves and guards well that which is good and worthy, so vile and base is that man who considers only his own well-being and social standing and sacrifices all for his own interest. He has no right to put his prejudices before truth, his interests before the public welfare, his foolish routine before the ministry of God. It is a crime against God and man, a crime against the Holy Spirit, that sin which "will not be forgiven" (Matt. 12:31). The priests were "preservers" in this sense: they boasted of Moses, but for them Moses meant power, honor, and profit, and so they quoted him frequently. They were the champions of the established order, the guardians of the existing state of things. To be on good terms with the Romans, to maintain their own influence over the people, to live publicly and make a great show — that was all their object. Religion was for them not an end but a means. Moses was not their master but their tool. As to the Messiah, of Him they seldom thought. He was for them a pure abstraction;

or if they did deign to say they were awaiting Him, they looked forward to Him only as One from whom they might derive some glory or benefit.

Such were the priests at the time of the ministry of Jesus. And side by side with this sacerdotal authority was the power of science. Doctors, scribes, almost all of them Pharisees—which is to say "separated," "distinguished"—men of one book, the Book of God, on which they made an only-too-human commentary; narrow, obstinate men, puffed up with pride, who sneered at and despised any who had not acquired "true knowledge," as they said, and "understood nothing of God's ways."

For them, salvation lay in a multitude of observances, which they catalogued as an apothecary does his recipes. They taught that morality was a code and religion a process. If you did not follow the recipe, you were lost. They maintained the *letter*, not the *spirit*, of the law. If you bought an egg that had been laid on the Sabbath, the gentle Hillel sent you to cook it in Hell!

In the Talmud we come across a curious classification, partly ironic and partly serious, which describes to a nicety the spirit of these men.

There are, we are told, seven kinds of Pharisees:

1. The "oppressed" Pharisee, who walks with his back bent, under the weight of the law, which he is reputed to carry on his shoulders.
2. The "covetous" Pharisee, who asks for payment before fulfilling a precept.
3. The Pharisee "with bleeding forehead," who walks with eyes cast down—as though from humility or shame—and knocks his head against the wall.
4. The "pretentious" Pharisee, who struts about in long, flowing garments.

5. The Pharisee "who works out his salvation," always seeking a good work, and who ever seems to be saying: "What is to be done, and I will do it."
6. The Pharisee who is moved by "fear."
7. The Pharisee who is moved by "love."

This last class certainly did exist, because we know that after the death of Jesus, such as these became eminent Christians; for example, St. Paul was a converted Pharisee, while from among the Sanhedrin came Joseph of Arimathea and Nicodemus.

But these latter were the exceptions. Taken in a block, the Pharisees were not of much value, except to themselves. Sacerdotal functionaries or professors of science, the scribes and the Pharisees possessed the same pride, the same contempt for the poor; they disguised and hid under the cloak of virtue the same avarices and the same vices. Haughty men, living on other men's virtues and betraying virtue in their hearts; shrewd judges, who imposed insupportable burdens on the consciences of others, which they would not raise a finger to remove — "whited sepulchers," as the Master called them, fair without and odious within — men, at once flattering and blood-thirsty.

We know them well, and well did Jesus know them! He said to them — under the porch of Solomon, facing the sepulchers on the Mount of Olives, which remain to this day — "You see those tombs: you are like them: without they are white, but within they are full of dead men's bones and corruption. You do well to decorate and venerate them, for you are like them. Your fathers killed the prophets who rest within them. You continue their work; truly you are their sons" (see Matt. 23:27–31).

Under these conditions, what sympathy could possibly exist between Jesus and the leaders of the people? Jesus with His liberty and truth, the priests and ancients with their craftiness and shame—it was an impossible position, and divorce was the only conclusion. What was no less of a certainty was that, in the rupture, the priests would take the initiative.

Think what a constraint He was! No means of deceiving Him; no way of hoodwinking the people. His clear eye pierced all their sophistry. The evidence of truth that showed itself in all He said drew to His side, almost unconsciously, all those whom they had striven so hard to gain. And then all the perfidies and unjust gains, the cruelties, the impieties that were committed within the walls of the Temple and were hidden and glossed over—all these He brought to light, and their deceit was laid bare. It was too much! They must silence and put down, at any cost, this uproar caused by the new Prophet before He became too powerful.

Thus, their state of mind is explained. They were seized with fear and bitten by a mortal jealousy, which roused all their forces against our Divine Savior. No scruple stopped them; no perfidy was beneath them. They sought false witnesses; they sent their spies to try to ensnare Jesus in His speech; they racked their brains for intricate questions with which to puzzle Him; they slipped in among the crowds that gathered around Jesus, and disseminated hateful calumnies against Him. "This is a man fond of good living." "He is the enemy of our country." "He practices witchcraft and has dealings with the devil." "His is an infamous doctrine, full of snares and darkness." And so forth.

And against all this opposition, what did Jesus do? Did He avoid all contact with them? That He could not do, for in order to do so, He would have had to leave the country, renounce His work, and let truth be silent. This was not possible. Would it be an acceptable gentleness that was bought at such a price?

Gentleness does not consist in not hating anything; still less does it consist in taking the side of wrong "for peace' sake" and not striving to cure it. That is indifference, and insipidity of soul; nowadays this trait is disqualified by the high-sounding name of dilettantism.

Dilettantism is odious because to its disciples, good and evil are of equal value; because, instead of a healthy dislike for weak, vile things, they who profess this cult have only a silly smile for all, and such conduct is mean and cowardly. Evil must be hated as intensely as good is loved. Jesus loved good. With all the vehemence of His human heart, and with the infinity of His divine nature, He loved it. What could He do? How could His pure eye contemplate these hypocrites, these men of gold and lip praise, these traitors? What could He set up in opposition to their shifty ways, which tended to stifle His work, and to close to others those gates of Heaven through which they themselves would not enter? He could do but one thing: unmask them, and, when the time came, set His foot on this nest of vipers, even at the risk of thereby meeting His own death.

This is the explanation of those expressions of anger that the Gospel relates concerning Jesus. There is naught thereat to be scandalized; rather would there be occasion for scandal were it not so, for it was His desire for the salvation of men that caused Him to condemn those who were obstacles in His path.

If He had pity for those who did wrong through weakness, He had only indignation against those who defended evil, who cultivated it, systematized it, turned it to profit. He hated their theories and conduct with a hatred born of His love of good, with a hatred that could cause the mild Lamb of God to be as fierce as the eagle and as furious as the lion.

Yes, truly it was love, love of His children, that roused in Him those transports of rage against any who would rob Him of their souls. From a flaming furnace of love, whence proceeded a devouring fire, His words derived their heat from the burning coals of divine charity.

But how terrible those words were! How terrifying His anathemas! At times His actions of anger might even seem exaggerated, as, for example, when He made a whip of little cords and expelled the buyers and sellers from the Temple. He overwhelmed the Pharisees, denounced them before God and man, and threatened them with terrible vengeance in His Name.

It was the cry of that love "strong as death," and of that jealousy "hard as hell," spoken of in the Canticle (Song of Sol. 8:6).

And all these threats and all the fierce anger of His divine manhood terminated in that piteous appeal of outraged love: "Jerusalem, Jerusalem, that killest the prophets, and stonest them that are sent to thee, how often would I have gathered thy children as the bird doth her brood under her wings, and thou wouldst not? Behold your house shall be left to you desolate" (Luke 13:34–35). The indignation of Jesus was one of His glories and His magnitudes, for He used it only in defense of justice and truth. His example has been followed in His Church, and it explains more than one crisis in the history of Christian civilization.

The scribes and the Pharisees still live; nor is Jesus Christ dead: He lives and acts in the Church He founded. The struggle is always going on, and the reason is the same. Authority is not necessarily a school of virtue. When power is held by weak, perverse men, it is sure to be their ruin. Although representing and containing Christ, the Church also contains many weak and erring children, and thus a struggle goes on and will do so for centuries to come. We must consider this conflict with calm observation and do all in our power to aid the work of good. All authorities and powers must rule over their own domain, and we can only earnestly deplore the scandals that arise at times in the very temple of truth itself. It is useless to deny them and to assert their impossibility would be to interfere in the freedom that God has left each creature to act for itself.

Long live truth, even when it wounds us!

These are but human accidents, which are naturally attendant on every person, who, though divine in one sense, is full of human imperfections. The root of the conflict is elsewhere, even as it was in the days of Jesus. Christ was opposed by the pride and injustice of the high priests; the Church still has pride and injustice to combat, and she must assert her independence. She may not bend the knee—before God, yes, but to man, never! She must speak openly and freely, whatever happens, for she holds, even amidst the universal turmoil, the noble bearing of faith and duty. Oh, this can chafe and irritate, this unswerving finger pointing ever at truth! It will not allow some wished-for success, because it is unjust, nor a certain mode of procedure that would lead to fame; and, again, it may open our eyes to the worthlessness of an easily won prize.

What is happening daily around us? False and unjust authorities form projects against the Church, even as they did against Christ. We cannot alter the course of events. Struggle is the normal state of truth upon earth.

Truth is like the knights errant of the old days of romance, who even lay down to sleep in armor, and never rested but on their lances.

The battle rages around us. For us, children of the Church, our duty is to take the right side in the conflict—our Master's side—and to cooperate, each to the best of his power, in the triumph of right.

Chapter 6

∞

Jesus and His Disciples

One word more than all others seems to express the attitude of Jesus toward His disciples. Men often attach to this word a meaning of restraint, even of contempt; but here we can use it in its fullest and highest significance. We mean the word *kindness*.

Kindness that bestows favors, kindness that stoops, kindness that helps, kindness that forgives, kindness that crowns all other gifts with the gift of self—this was the kindness that Jesus showed His chosen ones.

The first manifestation of this kindness, and the first relationship—if we may so speak—of Jesus with His disciples was their "vocation." We know how this happened; we read it in the Scripture, and it would seem at first glance as if Jesus gathered His fellow laborers at random. On the banks of the Jordan, after the testimony of John, two of his hearers, fishermen of Galilee, who were there earning their livelihood, approached Jesus.

He, turning and seeing them, said: "What seek you?" They answered: "Master, where dwellest Thou?" He said: "Come and see." They followed Him and remained with Him. The day following they sought Peter and John, and told them: "We have found the Messiah." They, coming, spoke with Jesus, and abode with Him (see John 1:35–42).

Again He met another, Philip, by the way and called him by the words "Follow me" (John 1:43).

A little farther on, as He was journeying through Galilee, He saw Nathanael sitting under a fig tree, and, calling him silently, He chose him as one of His disciples. Having arrived at Capernaum, and passing the custom house, He saw Matthew, the tax-gatherer, and called him.

And thus He called the others also.

Is there any need for us to say that all these seeming chances were ordained by divine knowledge and regulated by the sovereign will? Chance—to call it by its proper name—is the providence of God, and especially in what concerns the work of redemption, all is arranged, disposed, and adapted with a divine art and predilection. In order specially to designate them, Jesus gave to some of His disciples, when He called them, names characteristic of their special mission. He, as it were, prophesied with regard to them, and this prophecy it was that showed them that their vocation, instead of being given at hazard, was in reality ruled by divine choice.

A little later, when He desired to constitute His apostolic group, and to set down for each one his place and work, He passed the entire night in prayer on the mountain, and in the morning, returning to the borders of the lake, He proceeded to choose the founders of His Church—an example to us to seek for divine guidance in all our undertakings.

They were, in truth, weak and of little worth, these disciples. With the exception of one among them, who seemed to have a certain knowledge—and what a baneful knowledge!—they were all poor men, without power, without culture. They possessed nothing; they must receive all from their Master. But He was rich indeed! From the first day of their companionship with

Him, He made them rich, in opening up for them such glorious prospects in the future.

The future! How did it appear to the only-too-earthly eyes of the Apostles? What pictures did they paint of it? It would be hazardous to guess what they expected, but we know that they had not a correct idea of the kingdom of Christ. They were initiated, little by little; and slowly, step by step, they followed out God's designs. What matter for anxiety could they have? All the riches of the future were contained in the gentle call of Jesus to follow Him, even as all the leaf and flower and fruit are held in the tiny seed.

May we not safely conjecture that had these simple men known the greatness of their calling—the wondrous deeds they must do in the name of Christ—they would have been confounded at the disproportion between themselves and the great future before them? To be the founders and cornerstones of the Church, to cooperate with Him who is the Maker of the universe, to head the procession of the nations, who would march century after century, and only end when eternity begins—this was their destiny.

They did not know this; but one thing they knew that filled them with love and gratitude was that their work would bear fruit, that they would be the Fathers of the new Church. This was the title their Master gave them—the title He applied to Himself—spiritual Fatherhood. And is there in the world a more noble calling than to create again, as it were, souls for Christ?

St. Thomas Aquinas says that had the Creator alone given us our entire being, body and soul, He would have reserved to Himself His most wonderful power and most noble gift. But it did not please Him to act thus. He gave His creatures life, and the power to communicate life to others; to live and to cause to live; to act and to become the principle of action in other beings. That is why all paternity has in it something of the divine. This divine element in generation is the reason why the rejection of it is unreasonable as well as criminal. It is the reason why those vile profaners of that sacred tie that unites souls and bodies, who make of the divine institution of Christian marriage a selfish and shameless treaty, call down upon themselves the anger of Heaven and deserve the condemnation of men.

A man who can beget a work, either spiritually or naturally, which is beneficial to his fellow men and of service to his family or his nation, and who neglects this duty through unworthy and selfish motives, is contemptible and cowardly.

Thus, when God calls anyone, as He called His disciples, to a spiritual fecundity—to the communication of, and development of, divine gifts—such a one can never sufficiently bless His Master, never have enough delight in Him, never worthily serve Him.

Jesus taught His Apostles that they must appreciate their divine vocation. "You have not chosen me," He said; "I have chosen you" (John 15:16). As if to say, "Do not fancy that in coming to Me you have rendered me a favor; on the contrary, it is I who bestow the favor, and you who accept it. I have taken you to myself, and in taking you, I have favored you. You are honored in belonging to me. You shall be the channels through which shall flow the life I give to the world. In dispersing you over the world, as I shall do when I have returned to my Father, you will become as rivers, bringing life to the arid plains, as clouds dropping gentle, fructifying dews to the thirsty soul. You are the branches of the great Tree of which I am the Root, and the divine sap, mounting from me and spreading unceasingly, will cause the rich foliage to bud and break forth from you, like the tender

green shoots from the towering oak." Such was the meaning of
the call so simply given by Jesus to His Apostles, and we shall
see that this first grace, which no action of theirs merited, was
but the forerunner of others hitherto unknown to man.

∞

The first consequence of this call was intimacy between them
and Jesus. We must not wonder at receiving a certain shock on
first considering the intimacy between the Apostles and their
Divine Master.

Jesus Christ was man, the Universal Man, and it would appear that being so, He could not be especially intimate with
anyone. To live alone and within Himself would appear to
be the only position from which He could govern and direct
His work. Again, He was God, and on this account intimacy
with a creature would seem profane and undignified. What
intimacy could exist between God and men? Intimacy implies
equality; it is the mingling of lives; it is fraternity of hearts; it
is mutual transparency; it is closest union of soul and soul; it
is communication of thoughts, desires, ambitions, love, with
entire and reciprocal liberty to penetrate at any time, and to
any extent, into the motives and actions of each other. In this
sense, how could intimacy exist between Jesus the Man-God
and any of His creatures? His creatures are so small, so weak,
so foolish, so useless; and He is so ineffable, so far beyond this
life and this world.

It is the destiny of great minds to live alone, to let no other
penetrate into their inner selves, to call no one their intimate
friend. True, more than one genius has had friends, but no one
whose genius was of the highest order has had *intimate* friends.
The greatest of our men, whose genius stands out clearly to all

ages, such as Michelangelo, Shakespeare, Beethoven, Dante, and before these, again, those holy men Isaiah and Moses, had no familiar friends. They had confidants, they had protégés, satellites of their glory, followers of their work, servants whose devotion amounted to a very passion; but intimates—no! Their souls were too lofty; no other could inhale the atmosphere. They were as men marked with a terrible but sacred sign.

How far greater than all these men was our Divine Master! No human soul could compare with Him; no earthly thought could ever aspire to be even a reflection of His. Who could dare call himself simply His inferior, without at the same time holding himself up to ridicule? To be inferior to anyone is to compare oneself to him, and with Jesus comparison is impossible. His level? Infinity. His compass? Immensity. His thoughts? Those of God Himself. Who dare aspire to this intimacy? Who could live and thrive in that region of light? Who could gaze on that infinite horizon of perfection? No one.

This is all true, but God shows us other aspects of Himself—if we dare so speak—than His greatness. There is a divine condescension that shows, beside Jesus the immense stands Jesus the lowly, who emptied Himself of His glory and became like to us, Jesus who let Himself be held and handled and who was so great that He would not let us feel how poor and small we were. This is Jesus as we see Him with His Apostles.

Tradition tells us that Jesus hid the brightness of His eyes lest the glory of them, in shining on weak and wondering man, should hinder Him in His daily work. This, though, is certain: that He veiled the brightness of His soul and that He showed Himself to men only as the ever-watchful Father and kind and sympathetic friend. This was His attitude with His disciples. He made Himself, in a sense, their equal. He gave them sympathy and sought theirs. He held familiar converse with them, took part in their conversations, rejoiced and mourned with them.

When our Divine Savior would multiply the loaves in the desert, He turned and saw Philip beside Him, and knowing His disciple's simplicity, which He would put to the test, He said to him confidentially: "Philip, whence shall we buy bread that these may eat?" The Gospel tells us He said this to try him. And Philip fell into the trap. He said: "Two hundred pennyworth of bread is not sufficient for them, that every one may take a little" (John 6:5–7). This little conversation shows us how close was the intimacy between Jesus and His Apostles.

Again, we notice there was always a tinge of seriousness in His manner. We do not ever read that Jesus laughed. Laughter will at times arise from pride and ill feeling, and frequently it betokens want of control and amusement beyond one's power of will. Jesus smiled a smile of kindness, of encouragement — noble and genial — but He was always self-controlled, as befitted a master.

Generally His tone with His chosen ones was of a gentle tenderness, full of affection and simplicity. He called them His "friends," His "children," His "little ones," His "little flock" (see John 15:15; 21:5; Luke 10:21; 12:32). He explained to them apart the parables He had taught the people: "To you it is given to know the mysteries of the kingdom of Heaven, but to the others in parables" (see Matt. 13:11).

Often He drew them aside to be alone with them. On the roadside between one town and another He instructed them, He consoled them. He guarded them as a watchful parent, invited them to pause and rest when the way was long and their feet were weary, and prayed and blessed them while they slept.

At midday, when the burning Eastern sun became too hot and shot its fierce, blinding rays across the sandy plains, He drew them aside, under the spreading trees, or into a cool, shady grotto, and there, sitting in their midst, He discoursed to them so sweetly that they forgot all things while listening to His voice. And, His love overflowing, His yearning heart disclosed itself, and as the burning hours passed unnoticed, the disciples felt their souls flooded with a strange joy, and their spirits were soothed with a gentle peace as their hearts were invaded by that love, to which He could give no measure other than the love His Father bore Him. "As My Father hath loved me, so I love you" (see John 15:9). "He that heareth you, heareth me; he that despiseth you, despiseth me" (Luke 10:16). "And I say unto you, it shall be more tolerable at that day for Sodom than for that city that repulses you" (see Matt. 10:14–15).

There were times when His overburdened heart seemed almost to burst all bounds in its expressions of tenderness — not the weak, effeminate tenderness so common among men, but the strong, deep tenderness of a perfect human soul.

One day in particular, this may be noticed. He spoke to the crowd in the presence of the Pharisees, and His words were vehement and accusing. His disciples, as was their custom, stood close around Him, and in the midst of His discourse one among them said to Him: "Behold Thy Mother and Thy brethren without seek for Thee."

Hearing these words, His soul being filled with an intense emotion, He cried out: "Who are my Mother and my brethren?" Then, stretching His hands toward His disciples, He gazed on them with a look of unutterable devotion, and said: "Behold my Mother and my brethren; for whosoever shall do the will of God, he is my brother and my sister and mother" (Mark 3:31–35). Sublime gradation of tenderness, which from a union full of strength, the firm affection of a brother, passed to that tenderer, closer love so full of charm — the boundless ocean of a mother's heart!

This is the light in which we love to see our Master. We have our share in these transports of His love — we whom He calls to the intimate relationship of being His disciples. We are His friends, His brethren. To us also He says: "As My Father hath loved me, so I also love you." By the gift of His grace, which He has bestowed upon us, He forms a contract between us. We can call Him our Friend — our other self — without depriving Him of respect, without doing anything else than respond to the dearest longing of His heart. We can speak to Him in spirit, occupy ourselves with His interests, inquire into His mysteries, disquiet ourselves with a yearning for His glory. We have a right to the heavenly kingdom, which is now His kingdom, and which will be ours through Him. Our conversation is in Heaven, says St. Paul: *Conversatio nostra in coelis* (Phil. 3:20).

We have seen that the goodness or kindness of Jesus toward His chosen ones was manifested in the first place by calling them, and this was followed by the intimacy He established between Himself and them, but we notice this kindness most especially shown in the *patience* that He always exercised toward them.

He had great need of patience with these men, ignorant, uncouth, full of faults, as we all are — full of good intentions also, but weak and blind to a degree.

When His voice was raised in preaching, and His words revealed the divine truths He would teach them, they no longer understood Him, and they could think of Him and judge Him only from their natural standpoint. He preached to them humility, and yet they ever sought the first place; He taught them charity, and they asked if they might call down fire to consume the cities.

He strove to make them understand what He was doing—the spiritual character of His work, rather than the earthly idea the Jews had formed of the Messiah—but they held fast by their old opinions. "My kingdom is not of this world," said Jesus again and again (John 18:36). "The kingdom of God is within you" (Luke 17:21). "Labor not for the meat which perisheth, but for that which endureth unto life everlasting, which the Son of Man will give you" (John 6:27). They heard these truths repeatedly fall from His lips; they sounded in their ears, but glided over their souls, like seed blown over the rocks, and still they asked the old question: "When wilt Thou establish the kingdom of Israel?" (see Acts 1:6). When our Divine Savior taught His disciples what would come to pass concerning Himself—the Cross instead of the jeweled throne that they longed for—His confidences, instead of enlightening them, only confused them more. They listened attentively and reverently, but as men in a dream. "They understood not the word" (Mark 9:31). "Their eyes were held" (Luke 24:16). "They were amazed" (see Mark 1:27). How often we meet these expressions in the Gospel!

After some of these wonderful revelations their hearts were so troubled that they almost refused to believe in Him. We are told in St. Matthew's Gospel of this state of their mind, to which Peter, as their chief and leader, gave expression.

It was at Caesarea Philippi that Jesus announced His coming Passion, and how He must suffer at the hands of the ancients, and scribes, and priests, and be put to death. Peter dared to rebuke Him. He took our Lord on one side, and boldly said to Him: "Lord, be it far from Thee; this shall not be unto Thee." And Jesus, turning to Peter with unusual severity, said to him:

"Go behind me, Satan; thou art a scandal unto me, because thou savorest not the things that are of God, but the things that are of men" (Matt. 16:21–23). Poor St. Peter! He rejoined his brethren, downhearted and humbled; he felt the reproach so keenly, though he knew how kind was the heart of the Master who spoke it.

But it was seldom that Jesus spoke severely to His disciples. He was patient and forbearing with them. For all their miseries He had comfort, compassion, toleration, and He treated them with the fond indulgence of a Father. Even their faults and follies had no power to lessen His gentle loving-kindness.

Let us turn to another page of the Gospel, where we read of another fact; indeed, one of the most beautiful recorded of Jesus, and which is as a contrast to the circumstances just cited.

Jesus was alone. His disciples, grouped at a distance, were occupied in a discussion that, arising from human frailty, was an only-too-common one among them. They came to Him and asked Him the question that was troubling them: "Master, who thinkest Thou is the greater in the kingdom of Heaven?" As an answer to their query, Jesus called a little child, and set him in their midst, saying: "Whosoever shall humble himself as this little child, *he* is the greater in the kingdom of Heaven" (Matt. 18:1–4).

Beautiful picture! Worthy representation of the Son of God, who full of grace and truth, overflowing with kindness and love of little ones! We can fancy how frustrating these quarrels for preference and this seeking after the first place must have been to the King of Heaven. He felt their futility more than anyone else could, but these were His children, His little flock, for whom

He was about to give His life, and He bore with them, gently corrected them, and, not wishing to change them too suddenly from their natural to the spiritual state, He waited patiently.

Waited! How often God has to wait for man! Our foolish pride; our want of love; our niggardliness with Him from whom we have received all things; the eagerness we show over what excites our interest, often leaving duty to one side; the forgetfulness of God, who never for a moment can forget us—all these call for the long-suffering patience of our Father in Heaven, and still He waits. He stands at the door and knocks. He waits until we open our hearts; He gives us today what we refused to accept yesterday, and in the face of our coldness and our indifference, He continues to shower His graces upon us, as the glowing sun shines down on the frozen, snow-clad mountain.

Thus did Jesus act with His disciples. It was with gentleness that He drew them; He did not drive them with severity. He knew God's ways and He knew the ways of men, and He waited patiently till they were drawn to Him in perfect love. Meanwhile, He taught and consoled them. They were His chosen ones, and He stood at their hearts, seeking for a little opening whereby He might enter in. He would not force the entrance. He waited till they unlatched the door, and having entered in, He triumphed and reigned supreme. But still He waited and loved.

We come to the dark, slow days of the Passion.

The darkness was shed over the soul of Jesus. He drew His dear ones closer to Himself and took them, as it were, into His confidence. Oh, what gentleness, what patience He showed! He spoke to them for the last time on the eve of His death, after they had eaten the Pasch with Him.

The lights were low, and the shadows gathered around; an air of mystery and coming danger pervaded the little company. Jesus told them of the terrible prophecies about to be fulfilled, and then He consoled them with words of such tenderness that only the beloved disciple dared record them.

That night, His love for them was greater than it had ever been. He yearned to comfort them in advance, even forgive them, for the cowardice they would show on the morrow. He excused their faults—were they not His frail, feeble little ones?—and He could not bear to think of the remorse that would fill their hearts after they had deserted Him. With the tenderness of a loving mother, He drew them into His heart, and sorrowed for their sorrow when He should no longer be near to console them.

"Little children," He said to them, "yet a little while I am with you.... Whither I go you cannot come." And Simon Peter, his heart glowing with a spark from His Master's love, cried out: "Lord, why cannot I follow Thee?" And Jesus gently answered him whose burning love must yet be purified with humility: "Wilt thou lay down thy life for me? Amen, amen, I say to thee: the cock shall not crow till thou deny me thrice." Then He added, as though to console Peter and the others who heard: "Let not your heart be troubled. You believe in God: believe also in me." After a short time, seeing them penetrated with love, and the tears of tenderness stealing down their cheeks, He said to them: "Do you now believe? Behold, the hour cometh, and it is now come, that you shall be scattered every man to his own, and shall leave me alone; and yet I am not alone, because the Father is with me. These things I have spoken to you that in me you may have peace" (John 13:33, 37–38; 14:1; 16:31–32).

What kindness! What tenderness of heart! Like a fond father, who in the prodigal's departure sees only the dangers that beset him, and who calculates only the pain and remorse he will feel when his heart at length is broken, so was Jesus. The disciples were not haughty or malicious, only very weak. He, so good, so patient, did not want to discourage them; He wished only to put them on their guard and warn them of their danger. "Let not your heart be troubled. When these things come to pass, remember my words, and know that while I am speaking my heart is yearning for you; so do not lose courage, but rise and trust in me." This is how our Master loved us, one and all.

But what can we say when we glance at Judas—Judas, one of the twelve; one of those of whom Jesus said, "I will not call you servants, I will call you friends" (see John 15:15)? Unhappy Judas! He betrayed his Master for thirty pieces of silver. And Jesus knew it. For three years He kept this secret to Himself. He treated Judas like the rest; called him, trusted him, heaped upon him countless benefits. No one—unless, perhaps, John, whose love for Jesus seems to have penetrated the traitor's guise—could have suspected that Judas was he whom Satan had chosen as his tool. Our Savior even gave him a special mark of confidence: He entrusted him with the money belonging to the little band. But Judas was avaricious. John perceived this. Jesus appeared to close His eyes to this and left time and grace to do their work.

And over this heart, which slowly and firmly closed its doors, Jesus showered the gifts of love, and again and again offered pardon—that gift so rare among men—so precious that they hesitate to accord it to the sinner. How mysterious is the attitude of Jesus toward the traitor! More than anything else, it shows to what an excess His love for man could go.

Jesus and His Disciples

Jesus drank deeply, slowly, silently of that royal cup of sorrow — treason from a friend, from one who was nearer than a brother. And all the time, He heaped benefits on the fallen Apostle. He spoke to him kindly, gently, having always before His mind the treason Judas sought to conceal. He washed Judas's feet the night before He died, and when He had been already sold by him. In the Garden of Gethsemane, when at last the traitor threw down the mask and put the crown on his infamies by the betrayal kiss, Jesus said to him, in the old familiar tone of love, "Friend, whereto art thou come?" (Matt. 26:50). He still called him "friend." He wanted to show Judas that he, even he, had not exhausted the love and patience of His heart. Surely this scene is the climax of the love that Jesus had for His disciples. It lays bare a horizon so vast that the eye of man cannot fathom it, for the heart that was open to the traitor Judas is open still for all sinners. They are all lost in this abyss of mercy, and the call for the prodigal's return is ever sounding in their ears.

After He had left His chosen ones, Jesus would give them another assurance of His love.

He called them to a sublime vocation. He admitted them to an intimacy that astounded them. He bore with them and suffered mistrust and coldness from them without diminishing His love. Then, when He must leave His little flock, He sent His Holy Spirit to complete the work that He had begun in their souls.

Yet even then His heart was not content; His love was not satisfied. To crown all, to make their vocation more sublime, to render their intimacy with Him more real, to perfect the patience that He had taught them by His example, to add yet another jewel to their diadem of glory, to let them give Him what, in love, He had given them, He gave them what only He could give—all powerful as He was—to those He loved best: He offered them the martyr's crown, allowing them to die for Him.

Chapter 7

∞

Jesus and Nature

∞

Nowadays men ascribe great importance to the influences of Nature. The bonds between man and the earth that gave him birth — whence every day he derives existence and to which he will one day return — these bonds are the subject of frequent discussions in science; but, unfortunately, as is generally the case with human thought, exaggeration has crept in, and men attribute too much to this influence of Nature and make it responsible for all that befalls us.

Our will, our reason, and, above all, the action of God are forgotten. With relation to Jesus Christ, those who regard Him as only a perfect man, and nothing more, and apply the principles we have just mentioned to Him err in an even graver manner.

We read their beautiful descriptions of Palestine on the one hand, and then, on the other, their eulogy on the character of Jesus. They tell us that His surroundings were responsible for the grace and beauty of His soul. They forget that the same Galilee, whence came the gentle Lamb of God, was the most turbulent of the Roman provinces; nor do they mention that many of the seditions and revolts had been nurtured in the very caves that later echoed with the peaceful accents of the Sermon on the Mount.

But we will let these errors pass and sift out the truth of the principle. We will see how Jesus was in touch with the Nature that surrounded Him and how Nature itself had a prominent place in His life and teaching.

We have already seen, with regard to the human soul of Jesus, and also His ministry, how much can be justly attributed to Nature—first, as to the formation of His humanity, and secondly, as to its manifestation. Nature did not create Jesus, but it contributed to make Him as men saw Him. He proceeded from God as His Father, but for Mother He had Mary, and through Mary He became one of the human race, a child of this earth, a native of a certain place, and subject to certain external influences of association and climate. It would have been miraculous had this not been so, and God does not work miracles without a reason.

We must be careful not to exaggerate these influences. Above all, Jesus was what He wished to be, and what it was necessary that He should be for the perfect fulfilment of His mission; but there was no reason why He should not, at the same time, be a natural child of His country. Even as every flower that grows and blooms in its native soil owes to that soil certain qualities as to its size, shape, color, and scent, so is it with men, and so also with Jesus. Within Himself, He contained everything, and no power could act on Him without His will; but we have seen in His preaching and in His dealings with men certain characteristics that can be traced to His natural surroundings.

Although we speak of Jesus as the Universal Teacher and say that while speaking to His little flock, He was preaching to the whole world, still, we must also say that in His speech and words there was a certain originality. We use the word in its etymological sense—that is to say, it showed His origin, His individual nationality, His native tastes. Why was this? The

answer is obvious: Because a man's speech is always an expression
or reflection of the man, and a man must necessarily be more or
less colored by his surroundings.

A thought does not come out of our minds just as it is formed.
On the way, it passes through our imagination, which lends it
certain individual coloring, which is furnished, firstly, by our
heredity, and secondly, by our environments.

The imagination is like a living reservoir that stores within
itself certain forms, sounds, colors, impressions, memories, and
so forth, with which again it clothes our thoughts as they leave
our minds. This process took place in Jesus Christ, as in all men.
His imagination was ruled, controlled, and ordered more carefully
than is the case with us; but, still, it was there, with all its powers. All forces of Nature made certain impressions on Him; they
affected Him as they do us, only they were in a greater measure
controlled by His will. They were as food that nourished His
mind, in the same way that the food He ate nourished His body.

What, then, were the feelings of Jesus toward Nature? To begin
with, it follows logically that as He could understand Nature
more perfectly than we can, so He must have loved it more.
That which makes Nature so lovable is the beauty that we see
in it. Also, we are drawn to it by a certain harmony that seems
to exist between it and us.

Nature, in a sense, is our mother. Our strength is derived from
her, and we are ever feeling her influence. Thus, to admire and
love Nature is, as it were, to admire and love the source whence
we have sprung, and we do this with the more pleasure and sympathy as we study it more. Does it not follow that, in Jesus, this
love must have been most intense, and that His humanity, while

finding in Nature a channel of communion with His Father, also derived from it most exquisite and intimate delights?

Jesus was, indeed, if we may so speak, well placed to appreciate the beauties of Nature. The little corner of the earth that Heaven stooped down to sanctify was one of the loveliest of the countries of the world. No country was ever more loved, and many were the reasons for this devotion—a devotion that even the prophets expressed in passionate cries of praise, and their natural appreciation of beauty had a great part in causing them to extol their fatherland.

"The Promised Land" was not an empty name, nor was "the land flowing with milk and honey" merely a figure of speech. Every Israelite was proud of his beautiful country, and in the days of Jesus, it was at the zenith of its beauty and development. It was not, like the Bosporus or the isles of Greece, a land of luxury and idle voluptuousness; it was a strong, healthy land, overshadowed with the dim mist of sadness.

The heat of the Eastern sun, which shone on Palestine in all its radiance, was tempered by the cool waters that intersected the country, and this combination caused the most pleasant climate possible.

In the first warm days of springtime work began, and around every lake and river sprang up a paradise of verdure. The Jordan, running down the land, shed life and prosperity as it flowed, and numerous canals covered all parts of the country. A huge valley dipped from south to north, like a vast carriage drive, and the banks of the river, protected from the winds and storms, and many feet below the Mediterranean, were like one large tropical garden.

Each season seemed to add fresh beauty to the land. The palm trees spread their waving leaves; the balsams—spoken of by Solomon—filled the air with their sweet perfume; the fruitfilled orchards flourished by the flowing waters and gave Jericho, in particular, a reputation over the whole world. Houses and palaces nestled among the gigantic palm trees, and their clear whiteness shone out in striking contrast with the verdant vegetation.

Above, on the hills and in the plains between the hills, a cooler temperature existed, and the flat tablelands were noted for their luxuriant harvests. Such were the lands of Galilee and Samaria, where Jesus lived. It is true that the land of Judah — properly called Judea — had neither fruitfulness nor gentle charm. It seems as though God would draw a visible distinction between the country where good tidings came to men and the land where the voice of God should be silenced.

This country was mountainous, and water was scarce. The earth was rocky and scarcely covered with soil; indeed, the ground was like a body of only skin and bone. The aspect of this part of the land was sad. It was said that to see Jerusalem planted high in the midst of barren, wild plains seemed as though Mount Moriah, on which the Temple stood, in falling from Heaven into the great gray cavern, caused such a commotion as to break the earth into rocky waves all around.

The Canticle of Canticles employs an expression that aptly describes this country: "Behold, my Beloved cometh, leaping on the mountains, skipping over the hills" (Song of Sol. 2:8). This was in reality what a traveler had to do in order to arrive at Jerusalem.

Perhaps this very ruggedness had in it a certain charm. It broke up the monotony of the scene, which otherwise might have palled from its calm serenity and which had about it the atmosphere of a dreamland. Certain it is that all this contributed to produce in Judea poets of high ideas and aspirations, whose descriptions of Nature surpass any to be read in our day.

More than any other, Jesus delighted in all these varied beauties of His native land. He loved the country that had provided Him with a birthplace, and in proportion to the perfection of His own nature He was sensible of the beauties of Nature around Him. He who said on the banks of the lake, "Behold the lilies of the field, how they grow," gazed with fond pleasure on these stately flowers, and praised them higher than the riches of Solomon (Matt. 6:28–29).

How He loved the fields and the work of the fields! How often He brought them into His parables! He loved the mountains and the lakes, the many-colored flowers, with their thousand scents—in a word, He loved all living Nature, that glory of the earth that proves and symbolizes the glory of God. As He went on His way, doing good to all, He did not disdain to gaze on, and to delight in, the treasures that Nature strewed along His path, as we poor, feeble imitators scatter blossoms in the path of His Eucharistic processions.

Two roads in particular were frequented by our Divine Master: the roads that lay between Jerusalem and Galilee, which two places were the headquarters, so to speak, of His apostolic ministry. One thing may be noticed with interest concerning the journeying of Jesus: it usually took place in the springtime. Of course, He was ever ready to go to the succor of His creatures and was always doing good to all—on the hottest day of summer just as in the deepest winter snow. We can picture Jesus in the rain and storm and biting wind looking for the lost and straying sheep, and again we see Him sitting, thirsty and weary, by the side of Samaria's well, scorched by the fierce summer sun: *Quaerens me sedisti lassus.*[2]

---

[2] "Faint and weary, Thou hast sought me," from the hymn "Dies Irae." —Ed.

But it was the Eastern custom not to travel much in the two extreme seasons of winter and summer—these were times of rest in the Jewish life—so we may conclude that Jesus traveled little at these times; in fact, His journeys to Jerusalem were generally at the time of the great feasts: the Pasch, Pentecost, and the Feast of Tents.

He journeyed in the early morning, so as not to interrupt His ministry, traveling on foot through the villages, preaching and curing, gathering other disciples as He went along, and profiting by the quiet twilight hours to whisper to their hearts and draw them into closer communion with Him.

Passing out of Nazareth or Capernaum, He descended into the deep valley we have spoken of, walking along the banks of the Jordan, where the willows and the red laurel dip their branches into the stream, and where the rippling of the water jingles with soft echo through the hills. Here he paused and preached to the villages on either bank of the river, crossing the shallow streams by the stepping stones that served as bridges, or, where the water was deep, by the fishing boats of His disciples. Then, having come to the borders of the Dead Sea, which crouched in its blackness at the foot of the giant Moab, He left the river's bank and passed on to Jericho, following, by a series of rocky paths, that famous Pass of Adummim, where the ruddy hue of the soil calls back to our minds the parable of the Good Samaritan. Making a last halt at Bethany, in the house of Lazarus, He entered the city of Jerusalem by the Garden of Gethsemane.

Often He took the road that lay through Samaria, the most frequented by pilgrims from Galilee to Jerusalem for the feasts, the same road along which He had traveled three times a year during those eighteen years of His hidden life and where He had been lost by Mary and Joseph at the age of twelve.

This road, on leaving Nazareth, ran along the Plain of Esdraelon, the veritable vineyard of Palestine. In the spring, this plain was one waving flag of verdure, where flowers and trees mingled in perfect harmony to form a matchless mosaic, while Tabor rose in majesty above and guarded it on the right. To the left stood the mountain of Gilboa, which echoed with the warning prophecies of the witch to Saul (1 Sam. 28); on the side of the hill, protected by a rampart of giant, thorny cactus, nestled the village of Nain, where Jesus raised to life the widow's son (Luke 7:11–16); farther on stood Shunem, full of the memory of the prophet Elijah (2 Kings 4); next En-Gannim, the city of the ten lepers mentioned in the Gospel (Luke 17); beyond lay Dothan, where Joseph was sold by his brothers (Gen. 37:17, 28), and which is still a resting place for caravans journeying to Egypt; then came Samaria, the ancient capital of Israel; then Sichem, with its rich gardens, its beautiful valley, its Temple perched on Gerizim, and separated from Jerusalem by the Samaritan valley; then came Jacob's well, where Jesus sat, weary and lonely, waiting for the Samaritan woman, and where, resting His eyes on the valley below, He said those beautiful words: "Behold, I say to you, Lift up your eyes, and see the countries, for they are white already to harvest" (John 4:35); a little farther on in the valley lay Silo, where the Ark rested; then Bethel, where Jacob saw the ladder rising to Heaven (Gen. 28:12). And thus, after four days' march, the traveler comes to Mount Scopus, where Jerusalem lies like a panorama stretched out before him.

The old rabbis said: "God bestowed on the world ten measures of beauty, and of these He gave nine to Jerusalem." No doubt it was on this spot they stood when they made this declaration. Truly it would have been difficult to find a more beautiful scene. Many a time Jesus, worn out with fatigue after His journeying, sat here on a rock and gazed with sorrow and loving admiration on Jerusalem, thinking of the troubles and humiliations in store for her. Today, walking along the paths that Jesus walked, and filled with memories of Him, one cannot help regretting that these places have lost much of their beauty and charm. Islam has here spread its fatal winding sheet, as it has done over all the countries it governs. The beautiful forests have disappeared, cultivation is scanty, the valleys are filled with weeds; instead of vineyards, hayfields, and plantations of olive trees in terraces, as in the days when the psalmist sang of the hills that were springing with gladness, the pastures that were filled with sheep, and the whole land was one grand cry of joy, desolation is spread over all. The aqueducts are broken; the people starve in idleness; the earth, parched by the sun, gasps vainly for a drop of water wherewith to be refreshed and cries out for the hand of the husbandman that would cause it to produce again its riches.

Choked with briars, suffocated with useless vegetation, where the thistle — symbol of ruin and decay — raises its head defiantly, the whole land, instead of uttering the cry of joy described by the psalmist, wails out a wild reproach to man, who has despoiled it of its beauty.

And yet Palestine is still dear to us; it is still the Holy Land. We love to visit and to contemplate it, and as we cannot clothe it again in its former grace, we embellish it in our imagination. Its form has not changed; the hills and valleys still remain; and we picture our Savior climbing the mountainside, and walking in the plains, sometimes silently praying, at other times conversing with His disciples, and all the while letting His eyes drink in the beauty of the scene around — a scene of such grace and vigor that it makes our cold streams and windy northern heights look like dark engravings beside a glowing picture.

And the heart of the Master grew glad as He gazed. Let us rejoice with Him, and then, strange as it may seem, even the present desolation will hold a charm.

As our eyes wander over the broad waste, where we see nothing but light, and color, and lifeless form—no animation, as it were, no soul, nothing to distract or delay our imagination—the dream of the past becomes more real. The mind has freer scope, the majesty of solitude seizes on the soul. The great silence enters like a river and floods the spirit. Vague murmurs rise around us from the rocks and vales, and by degrees the present fades away and we live again—one alive among the dead—in the glad bright days of the past, when Jesus, "the most beautiful of the sons of men," gazed on the beauty around (Ps. 44:3 [45:2]).

And thus, under the influence of a holy dream, our conscious being sleeps. We are borne away from things that drag us to earth, and we soar on the wings of love. Our pitiful personality is lost, and we live again in the days of our Master, seeing the land, not as now, a torrid waste, but full of richness and beauty.

But we must not stop here when considering the relations between Jesus and Nature. It would be erroneous to admit that He looked on it merely with an artist's eye. Even for us art is only a sublime amusement. It is a pure, elevated pleasure, but it is a vain joy if it does not lead to something higher. To be of real value, it must raise us above earthly things, and, like a ray of sunlight, it must be a clear, bright passage from beautiful creation to the source of beauty: God Himself. This was what Jesus realized and practiced to the full.

A threefold homage rose in His soul toward God when He gazed on Nature. He saluted God as the Creator. His thoughts rose and pierced the centuries of time to that first hour, when all life came forth from the bosom of God, where each being, no matter how small, was called its name by that Voice that gives existence to all things and when each little being was blessed.

And then, without needing to reflect on the past, He saw at that moment every creature held up and sustained by God, all life being drawn from that Source, all activity proceeding from Him, all riches flowing from the abundance of His riches, all Nature like a breath emanating from the divine mouth.

God alone exists by Himself. When He named Himself, He proved His right to be. He is "He who is." All other beings have only a finite existence, a borrowed life, and they depend on the one Infinite Being. As the ray of light depends on the sun as its center and source, so do we and all Nature depend on God.

Jesus regarded Nature thus, and that contemplation, after drawing His mind from Heaven down to earth, raised it again, to rest at length in God. He followed the ray of light from the creature to the Creator. But God is not only the Creator and Support of all creatures: He is also their model. No beauty charms us that is not a reflection of His beauty; no grandeur impresses us that is not an image of His greatness. God! It is He — His beauty, His strength, His wisdom, His goodness — that all voices and all echoes of this world proclaim. All times, all beings, all creatures cry out at once in stammering accents that name that the Hebrews dare not utter.

Each being is a note in the song of praise to God. The light has its notes, so also has the darkness. In those Eastern nights that Jesus loved so much, and in which He prayed His lonely prayer — in those bright sunlit hours, whose majesty was like a reflection of His sinless soul, wherein reposed the tranquil glory of the Heavenly Father, always He gazed with love on His dear earth; while high and low, up and down the ladder of Creation, from the great elements to the tiny insects, from weakness to strength, all chanted the praises of God, all proclaimed His glory, and all extolled the grandeur, the beauty, the power and the magnificence of the one great universal Creator of all.

But here we come to another mystery: Jesus Christ was Himself God—not only God, but the wisdom of God, the beauty of God, mirror of the perfections of His Father; "the brightness of His glory, the figure of His substance," as St. Paul says (see Heb. 1:3); the Word, spoken of by St. John—the living Word, which utters all things to God and of God.

Thus Jesus Christ, considered as God, as the Second Person of the Adorable Trinity, is Himself the Universal Model and Example, the Type of all being, the Substantial Idea of the Father, who in Himself comprises all Nature, and by whom, in consequence, all Nature exists. This, then, is a mystery; but is it not all a mystery? Jesus Christ unites within Himself God and man, the admiration of Nature and the control of Nature. He gazes on it, as it were, from without, and yet He produced it. He is its Model, and He finds pleasure in the resemblance. He regards Nature, then, in a twofold manner: as a spectator and, from within, as the creative idea, one with the Father, God Himself.

Thus, as He saw all things come forth from God, all reflect Him, He also saw all things reflected *in* Him.

Creation is a circle. God commences it; His work develops under the empire of the laws He dictates; it makes its way gropingly over all obstacles, and, after weary journeying, returns, like a tired child, back to its Father's arms. All Nature works for the Creator. All must be consummated in Him, in the completion of a perfect and unchangeable organization. Jesus knew that this would be. He saw Nature as God's workman — mysterious workman of a still more mysterious work — understood only by God Himself, and directed by Him.

Fénelon has said, "Man works and God directs," and so, also, Nature works and God directs.

In the great force that rules the vast heavens and threw into space the millions of stars, as in the growth of the smallest flower by the roadside, Jesus saw the providence of God, and He united Himself to it. He saw His place on earth as the Master of Nature, even as St. Paul says: "All things are made subject to the elect, and the elect are subject to Christ" (1 Cor. 15:27).

This is what Jesus saw and loved in Nature, and the great vision of the providence of God followed Him always. In every small detail of His daily life, it was His strength.

Can we realize how Jesus, with His immense soul, could take an interest in the little everyday trifles among which He lived, had His gaze not been directed toward infinite immensities worthy of Him? The thought of God's ever-watchful providence was His support in His labors, His joy in His sufferings, and He wills that this should also be our joy and our support.

O blind ones! O ye of little faith! "Why are you troubled? Are not two sparrows sold for a farthing? And yet not one of them shall fall without the permission of My Father. Are you not of more value than a sparrow?" (see Matt. 10:29, 31).

Thus we see our Divine Master, in gazing on Nature, considering the end for which man was made. Instead of the troubled pessimism of our day, which morbid poetry squeezes out of the beauties around us, and which dries and hardens the soul, Jesus flooded the minds of His disciples with a deep, abiding peace. He made them look with the clear gaze of faith and love on their fellow creatures around them, the earth, the slave of man, which gives him so much pleasure and pain, the sea and sky, the flowers and birds, all Nature working in unison under the one great power: the providence of God. This is what He taught His disciples; indeed, was this not the foundation of their belief and of all Christian belief—confidence in God, our Father?

We have come forth from God, and we cannot find rest until we return to Him.

We are the image of God, and we must see Him and honor Him in all.

We are returning to God. Separated only by a thin veil, which death, with ruthless hand, will tear aside, let us hold ourselves in readiness, and instead of living our lives carelessly, as it were by chance, without control or effort, let us walk ever watchfully in the footsteps of our Master.

We must live out our allotted time, not thoughtlessly, like the beasts and birds, not rebelliously, as, alas, we have so often done, but trustfully and manfully, doing God's will.

His will alone will prevail, and let us so act, so live, that it be ever accomplished in us, and lead us at last to the feet of our Father, where, with Jesus, we shall adore that Divine Will through the ages to come.

∞

Antonin Gilbert Sertillanges
(1863–1948)

Born in the French city of Clermont-Ferrand on November 16, 1863, A. G. Sertillanges entered the Dominican order twenty years later, taking the religious name Dalmatius. In 1888 he was ordained a priest.

After completing his studies and teaching for a few years, Fr. Sertillanges was appointed secretary of the prestigious scholarly journal *Revue Thomiste*. In 1900 he became professor of moral theology at the Catholic Institute in Paris, where he taught for twenty years. Later, Fr. Sertillanges taught elsewhere in France and also in Holland. During his year-long stay in Jerusalem in 1923, he was inspired to write *What Jesus Saw from the Cross*.

His classic book *The Intellectual Life* explains the methods, conditions, habits, and virtues that are necessary in the intellectual life. These virtues bore great fruit in Fr. Sertillanges's life, enabling him to become a widely recognized expert in the philosophy of St. Thomas Aquinas and to write many books and more than a thousand articles in the areas of philosophy, theology, art, and spirituality.

But Fr. Sertillanges was far more than a professor and a scholar. During his lifetime, he was widely admired for his skill as a preacher, a spiritual director, and an apologist, and was particularly successful in presenting the Faith in compelling terms to the young and to the unconverted.

Fr. Sertillanges was no "ivory tower" intellectual, but first and foremost a passionate son of the Church. His numerous works bridge the gap that often yawns today between academic theology and the everyday faith of the ordinary layman.

The fruit of both hard study and devout prayer, and motivated by the desire to preach Catholic truth *usque ad mortem* ("unto death," in the words of the Dominican motto), the works of Fr. Sertillanges are now informing and inspiring yet another generation of readers in these times of theological uncertainty and moral disarray.

Sophia Institute

Sophia Institute is a nonprofit institution that seeks to nurture the spiritual, moral, and cultural life of souls and to spread the Gospel of Christ in conformity with the authentic teachings of the Roman Catholic Church.

Sophia Institute Press fulfills this mission by offering translations, reprints, and new publications that afford readers a rich source of the enduring wisdom of mankind.

Sophia Institute also operates two popular online Catholic resources: CrisisMagazine.com and CatholicExchange.com.

Crisis Magazine provides insightful cultural analysis that arms readers with the arguments necessary for navigating the ideological and theological minefields of the day. *Catholic Exchange* provides world news from a Catholic perspective as well as daily devotionals and articles that will help you to grow in holiness and live a life consistent with the teachings of the Church.

In 2013, Sophia Institute launched Sophia Institute for Teachers to renew and rebuild Catholic culture through service to Catholic education. With the goal of nurturing the spiritual, moral, and cultural life of souls, and an abiding respect for the role and work of teachers, we strive to provide materials and programs that are at once enlightening to the mind and ennobling to the heart; faithful and complete, as well as useful and practical.

Sophia Institute gratefully recognizes the Solidarity Association for preserving and encouraging the growth of our apostolate over the course of many years. Without their generous and timely support, this book would not be in your hands.

www.SophiaInstitute.com
www.CatholicExchange.com
www.CrisisMagazine.com
www.SophiaInstituteforTeachers.org